PRODUCTIVE LABOUR
AND EFFECTIVE DEMAND

By the same author
Population Theories and the Economic Interpretation

PRODUCTIVE LABOUR
AND
EFFECTIVE DEMAND

Including a Critique of
Keynesian Economics
by
SYDNEY H. COONTZ

With an Introduction by
WILLIAM J. BLAKE

LONDON
ROUTLEDGE & KEGAN PAUL

First published in 1965
by Routledge & Kegan Paul Ltd
Broadway House, 68–74 Carter Lane
London, E.C.4

Printed in Great Britain by
C. Tinling & Co. Ltd.,
Liverpool, London and Prescot

CONTENTS

*Owing to production delays
this book was not published until 1966.*

ERRATA

page ix, *line* 13. Delete comma after 'ever known'.

    13, *note* 31. Insert question mark at beginning
                         of footnote.

   111, *line* 5.   To read 3·5:1.

Productive Labour and Effective Demand

ACKNOWLEDGEMENTS

I AM INDEBTED to Robert Edminster, Laurence Nabers and Ernst Randa for many helpful suggestions. Maurice Dobb was kind enough to read an earlier draft. I hope I have profited from his suggestions for improvement.

My greatest debt is to my dear friend William Blake who gave unstintingly of his time and constantly encouraged me throughout the project. The debt has been compounded by his introduction. However, as the reader will note, we didn't resolve one theoretical difference!

INTRODUCTION

by William J. Blake

THERE HAVE BEEN many studies of what constitutes productive labour and what constitutes effective demand. In this study Professor Coontz has treated these as faces of the same coin. While it is true that the relationships between these two aspects have often been treated in political economy, their cohesion has not received adequate treatment, even from giants like Ricardo and Marx.

Frequently their connection has been ignored, sloughed off, or even contradicted. In the two cases so elaborately studied here, of Malthus and Keynes, the advocates of unproductive expenditure, as creating effective demand, have impeached the very centre of this relationship.

The historic study of theories of productive labour and effective demand begins with the precapitalist theoreticians, who, naturally, thought of productive labour generally in ethical terms. The rise of a rudimentary capitalism focused the attention of theoreticians on trade and the transfers of specie from state to state, the more obvious and theatrical aspects of economic life, at a time when productive powers in industry were as yet feeble. From this point on, the development of productive forces in the eighteenth century centred attention more on the process of production and on trade as the derivative aspect of economic life, whether in the study of the totality of national production, as with the physiocrats; or, in the study of the anatomy of economic life, as with Adam Smith. Theory took on a new stature. In Ricardo classical economy became mature, in that Ricardo came to a pessimistic conclusion concerning the destiny of class relations based on an intensive study of the essence of productive labour and its contradiction in the variations of effective demand. Although this pessimism was strangely made congruent with

Introduction

Say's Law of Markets, the implications of the contradiction observed by Ricardo could only lead to that greater depth of analysis in Marx. In the course of his pertinent historic sections, which are not introduced as a show of erudition, but as illustrating the development of theory as conditioned by changes in the productive mechanisms and their relevant social setting, Professor Coontz has done an admirable job of work. He is also to be thanked for calling attention to the pioneer understanding of Playfair on the dynamics of capitalism, and to Lauderdale on the saturation possibilities inherent in the relationship of these two aspects of economic life.

But the importance of this work does not reside in either the history of these theories, nor even in the admirable criticisms of the epoch-making work of Marx, nor of the far more doubtful interventions of Keynes and of his school. True, the most striking analytical section of the book is the Keynesian disaggregation in which there is a merciless study of the conception that unproductive expenditure can achieve an economic balance by disregarding the basic factor of cost. This analysis is made in terms of the relationship of productive labour and effective demand, and to me seems conclusive.

The Marxian studies are more comprehensive. Marx paid a great deal of attention to sectorial analysis, the second volume of *Capital* being largely concerned with the interrelations of Sector One, producer goods and Sector Two, consumer goods. Despite the objections of Rosa Luxemburg whose treatment of this matter was *ad hoc*, Marx's contribution remains the starting point for sectorial analysis. But it has not received proper or adequate treatment in post-Marxian literature, whether by his disciples or his critics. Grossman, in his encyclopaedic study of Accumulation, deals elaborately with the possible variations of the two sectors, in revealing the shortcoming of Bauer's construction, and does, of course, point out that such imbalance is inescapable in a market economy. But what Grossman did not work out was not the question of what variations were possible, but which variations actually do take place. This want has been supplied in the present book.

Coontz has rightly centred his attention on the Great Depression. After pointing out that not one of the theorists on

Introduction

economic cycles, however distinguished, has made a genuine analysis of the cause of this most striking phenomenon of our century, he proceeds by way of sectorial analysis to ascertain to what extent the growth of the consumers' goods sector as related to the growth of the producers' goods sector acted as the determining factor in bringing about the Great Depression. This is not merely a refutation of naive under-consumptionism; it is the most significant treatment anywhere of the causative relationships of the growth of investment, employment, profits of the consumers' sector, as against that of the producers' goods sector. The impact of each sector upon the other and the culmination of these impacts in the outbreak of the greatest crisis ever known, revolutionize our understanding of the years 1929–40. I have not checked whether the American data, so conclusive for the United States, is as applicable to other countries, though for Britain it certainly seems so. However, as the United States, by its preponderant position in capitalism is a generating force well beyond its quantitative position, it is possible that even if this analysis were not so conclusive for countries with less economic weight, the Coontzian position would still be decisive. Nor can his study be ignored for its forecasting capacity. The developments since World War II are more than reminiscent of the sectorial aspects of the period preceding the Great Depression.

The final section, with its review of the many attempts to create effective demand without relation to productive labour, such as military expenditure, state capitalism, public works, while excellently stated, rather opens the door to further studies, as to the extent to which an inherent imbalance in a market economy must ultimately negate such interventions in their avowed purpose. It is to be hoped that Professor Coontz goes further in this fruitful field.

One difference: Coontz holds that Marx considered that services are as productive of surplus value as are material goods, given the relation of capitalist to the suppliers of labour power. His evidence, as here presented, seems decisive but I dissent on the basis of another synthesis.

WILLIAM J. BLAKE

Camberley, England

ix

For SHARRON and STEPHANIE

I

THE PRE-CLASSICAL APPROACH

(A) ANCIENT AND MEDIEVAL VIEWS

PRE-MERCANTILIST WRITINGS on political economy were primarily concerned with the development of a system of social ethics. Although in *The Republic* Plato recognized that retail trade is productive since it satisfies wants, nevertheless, as a representative of the aristocracy, he looked upon trade with disfavour. The ideal state would limit the numbers engaged in trade. Further, to the extent that trade was necessary, Plato expressed the wish there might be some method by which the morally better rather than the worse could be induced to follow the business.[1]

Aristotle distinguished between a natural economy—the science of household management—and an acquisitive economy. Exchange is natural in that it satisfies different wants. But exchange based on barter is superseded by trade which employs money as a means of exchange. Thus trade introduces corruption since money is transformed into capital. Money breeds money, and this is unnatural because money is sterile.

> There are two sorts of wealth getting . . . one is part of household management, the other is retail trade: the former necessary and honourable, while that which consists in exchange is justly censured; for it is unnatural, and a mode by which men gain from one another. The most hated sort, and with the greatest reason, is usury, which makes a gain out of money itself, and not from the natural object of it. For money was intended to be used in exchange, but not to increase at interest. And this term interest, which means the birth of money from

[1] *The Republic*, p. 64; *The Laws*, Book XI, pp. 470–1 in *The Works of Plato* (translated by B. Jowett).

1

money, is applied to the breeding of money because the off-spring resembles the parent. Therefore of all modes of getting wealth this is the most unnatural.[2]

Here there is a clear distinction between productive activity based on (proper) exchange of equivalents and the unproductive activity of money making.

Aristotle's approach to nascent market phenomena was institutional rather than economic:

> Whenever Aristotle touched on a question of the economy he aimed at developing its relationship to society as a whole. The frame of reference was the community as such which exists at different levels within all functioning groups . . . Community, self-sufficiency and justice were the focal concepts. . . . Trade is 'natural' when it serves the survival of the community by maintaining its self-sufficiency. The need for this arises as soon as the extended family grows overpopulous, and its members are forced to settle apart. Their autarchy would now be impaired all round, but for the operation of giving a share (*metadosis*) from one's surplus. The rate at which the shared services (or eventually, the goods) are exchanged follows from the requirement of *philia*, i.e. that the good-will among the members persist. For without it, the community itself would cease. The just price, then, derives from the demands of *philia* as expressed in the reciprocity which is the essence of all human community.
>
> From these principles derive also his strictures on commercial trading and the maxims for the setting up of exchange equivalencies or just price. Trade . . . is 'natural' as long as it is a requirement of self-sufficiency. Prices are justly set if they conform to the standing of the participants in the community, thereby strengthening the good-will on which community rests. Exchange of goods is exchange of services. . . . In such exchange no gain is involved; goods have their known prices, fixed beforehand. If exceptionally gainful retailing there must be for the sake of a convenient distribution of goods in the market place, let it be done by noncitizens.[3]

The medieval writers adopted Aristotle's views on usury but not on trade:

---

[2] *The Politics* (translated by ·B. Jowett).

[3] Karl Polanyi, 'Aristotle Discovers the Economy', in *Trade and Market in the Early Empires* (edited by Karl Polanyi, Conrad M. Arensberg and Harry Pearson), Glencoe, Illinois, 1957, pp. 79–80.

By a happy or unhappy fault, however, William of Hoerbeke in the translation of the *Politics* . . . rendered . . . the term for retail trade, as 'campsoria', a term with the specific meaning of money changing. Thus instead of being presented with a condemnation of all retail trade, which medieval Christian theologians would not have accepted, the early scholastics found in Aristotle only a condemnation of traffic in money; and themselves already suspicious of the *campsores*, they found this highly natural. Aristotle's case against usury, which rests largely on his case against all trade, is accepted by St. Albert and St. Thomas as simply a case against those who make money from money, a specialized and suspect group.[4]

Saint Augustine held that trade was licit 'unless carried on from mere lust of gain . . . also is the earning of a moderate gain, provided that the merchant transported the goods from another place to the market or to his store, where the consumers can obtain them'.[5] Ricardus de Media Villa (Richard of Middleton—*c*. 1249–1306) elaborated a utility theory of value as a justification for trade. Ricardus argued that the consumer derives a greater utility from what he purchases than from the money with which he parts. Similarly, the merchant obtains a greater utility from the money he receives than from the commodity he surrenders. In general, the idea of commutative justice prevailed, i.e. the equivalence of exchange. Unproductive labour was acquisitive, e.g. forestalling, engrossing, regrating, and the taking of usury.[6]

Scholastic analysis distinguished between productive and unproductive 'investment'. Productive capital was risk-bearing and hence entitled to a profit:

> He who commits his money to a merchant or craftsman by means of some kind of partnership does not transfer the ownership of his money to him but it remains his; so that at his risk the merchant trades, or the craftsman works, with it; and

[4] John T. Noonan, Jr., *The Scholastic Analysis of Usury*, Cambridge, Massachusetts, 1957, p. 47.

[5] M. Beer, *Early British Economists*, London, 1938, p. 31. Another medieval writer was of the opinion that the merchant must actually transform the commodity; but generally the mere transporting of the article was considered sufficient to entitle the merchant to a reward. *Ibid.*, p. 32.

[6] Besides commutative justice, medieval theorists believed in distributive justice, i.e. an individual should receive an income commensurate with the social status of his particular group.

therefore he can licitly seek part of the profit thence coming as from his own property.[7]

Noonan comments on this distinction as follows:

Why is risk used as the criterion of ownership . . . Above all, why is money considered to fructify in a partnership, and not in a loan? Why are the use and ownership of money distinguished in a *societas* and not in a loan? The failure to find any consistent answers to these questions in the first three centuries of analysis presages the disintegration of one part of the usury theory in the next three centuries. In fact, the early scholastics were working with two different theories on money, risk, and ownership, one of which they applied to loans, the other to partnerships. According to one theory, money was sterile, risk was no title to profit, ownership was the same as use in consumptible goods. In the other theory, money produced a surplus value, risk became the grounds for a reward, and ownership was determined not by the identity of use and ownership, but by the assumption of risk. Probably the greatest single difference in the two theories was in the treatment accorded to money, and this difference arose from money in loans being considered formally as a measure, while in partnerships money was tacitly identified with the goods it buys and not considered in its formal character at all. . . . In any event, the distinction as drawn, even by the medieval rigorists, left a wide field open for investment in business.[8]

Similarly in Jewish law, risk-bearing capital received legitimate profit, not interest. Thus, Maimonides (1135–1204) wrote:

A man is forbidden to give his money to another for the purpose of engaging in a joint venture on condition that he share in the profit but not in the loss, this being quasi usury. He who does this is called a wicked man. And if one gave money to another on such condition, they share the loss, as well as the profit, in accordance with the nature of their venture. He who gives his

---

[7] St. Thomas Aquinas, *Summa Theologica*, quoted by Noonan, *op. cit.*, p. 143.

[8] *Ibid.*, p. 152. In a footnote, Noonan correctly points out that 'The whole scholastic attitude towards *societas* is refutation of Tawney's rash assertion, "The true descendant of the doctrine of Aquinas is the labour theory of value. The last of the Schoolman was Karl Marx". (R. H. Tawney, *Religion and the Rise of Capitalism*, London, 1937, p. 36)'. *Ibid.*, p. 152, n. 50. As will be shown later, Neoclassical value theory is the true descendant of scholastic analysis!

money on condition that he share in the loss but not in the profit is called a pious man.[9]

Again, Muslim law based on the teaching of Abu Hanifah (*c*. A.D. 798) provides a risk justification for profit: in a limited partnership 'Each could enter into the business with equal or unequal shares, and arrange for an equal or unequal share in profits or losses.' In the sleeping partnership where one person supplied the capital and the other the labour, the 'essential condition was that profits should be common.'[10] Here risk of capital is equated with labour. In fact, the term 'risk' is of Arabic origin.

By the fourteenth century, Ibn Khaldun can quote with approval the hoary maxim of the merchant: 'Buy cheap and sell dear. There is commerce for you.'[11] Incidentally, Ibn Khaldun anticipates the classical economists' distinction between capital and revenue:

> (His) profits will constitute his livelihood, if they correspond to his necessities and need. They will be capital accumulation, if they are greater than (his needs). When the use of such accruing or acquired (gain) reverts to a particular human being and he enjoys its fruits by spending it upon his interests and needs, it is called 'sustenance'.[12]

Ibn Khaldun also anticipated the problem of effective demand:

> Now, if the ruler holds on to property and revenue, or they are lost or not properly used by him, then the property in the pos-

[9] Yale Judaica Series, Volume II, *The Code of Maimonides* Book Thirteen *The Book of Civil Laws* (translated from the Hebrew by Jacob Rabinowitz), New Haven, 1949, p. 95. The Hebrew term for usury is *nesek* (biting): 'Why is it called *nesek*? Because he who takes it bites his fellow, causes pain to him, and eats his flesh.' *Ibid.*, pp. 88–9. Similarly, '. . . Dante places the usurers in his "Inferno", not among the merely avaricious, but deeper down, among those guilty of crimes of violence; that was because they resorted to such shocking means to seize the persons and chattels of their victims. One of the men described by Dante belonged to a family which so despoiled an entire community as to cause a folk-uprising.' Miriam Beard, *A History of the Business Man*, New York, 1938, pp. 129–30.

[10] Von Kremer's, *The Orient under the Caliphs* (translated from the German by S. Khuda Bukhsh), Calcutta, 1920, p. 419.

[11] Ibn Khaldun, *The Muqaddimah* (translated from the Arabic by Franz Rosenthal), London and New York, 1958, Vol. II, p. 337.

[12] *Ibid.*, pp. 311–12.

session of the ruler's entourage will be small. The gifts which they, in their turn, had been used to give to their entourage and people stop, and all their expenditures are cut down. . . . the dynasty is the greatest market, the mother and base of all trade. . . . If government business slumps and the volume of trade is small, the dependent markets will naturally show the same symptoms, and to a greater degree. Furthermore, money circulates between subjects and ruler, moving back and forth. Now, if the ruler keeps it to himself, it is lost to the subjects.[13]

However, the ruler must be guided by the golden mean because excessive government expenditures mean heavy taxation which, in turn, discourages business as all hopes for profit are destroyed. In fact, Ibn Khaldun develops a 'Law of Civilization and Decay':

When civilization (population) increases, the (available) labour again increases. In turn, luxury again increases in correspondence with the increasing profit, and the customs and needs of luxury increase. Crafts are created to obtain (luxury products). The value realized from them increases, and, as a result, profits are again multiplied in the town.[14]

But now progress is negated:

The dynasty . . . soon starts to adopt luxury and luxury customs of a sedentary culture. . . . The result is that the expenses of the people of the dynasty grow. Especially do the expenses of the ruler mount excessively, on account of his expenditures for his entourage and the great number of allowances he has to grant. . . . Therefore, the ruler must invent new kinds of taxes. He levies them on commerce. He imposes taxes of a certain amount on prices realized in the markets and on the various (imported) goods at the city gates. . . . In later (years) of the dynasty (taxation) may become excessive. Business falls off, because all hopes (of profit) are destroyed, permitting the dissolution of civilization and reflecting upon (the status of) the dynasty. This (situation) becomes more and more aggravated, until (the dynasty) disintegrates.[15]

The medieval Christian world was also hostile to luxury expenditures and this hostility was based not only on the

13 *Ibid.*, pp. 102–3.
14 *Ibid.*, pp. 272–3.
15 *Ibid.*, pp. 91–2.

Church's other-worldly point of view—besides the ascetic condemnation, luxury was held to undermine the existing social order or hierarchy:

> . . . the feudal gentry made a great display of fine clothes but they were hard pressed by the ambitious burghers. Even royalty had occasion to be envious of townsmen, as when a Queen of France expressed her dismay at being outshone at a ball in Madegeburg by wives of businessmen, wearing toilettes sewn with pearls and emeralds and worth up to $400 (in modern money) apiece. It was also not unusual for high-born dames in local castles to stay home from tournaments because, as they fretfully told their liege lords, they had nothing fit to wear in the company of burgher women. . . . The rich traders of Thuringia, who wore little bells on their girdles that tinkled at every step, can hardly escape the charge of being a little *loud* in their dress.
>
> Sons of merchants knew no bounds to their extravagance and were undeterred by luxury laws or the railings of preachers. . . . Many moralizers of the times reprobated this restless craving. A popular preacher, almost an evangelist, Geiler von Kaiserberg, laments: 'In this world, no one wants to remain in the station given him by God; everyone wants to rise higher.' The kitchen-maid must dress like her mistress, the apprentice must wear furs; and 'the citizen will be a patrician, the patrician a Freiherr, the Freiherr a count, the count a prince, the prince a duke, the duke a king.'[16]

In summary, pre-mercantilist writers condemned both luxury and usury. Luxury was worldly and, moreover, threatened the established hierarchy. Usury constituted an illegitimate return to a *rentier*, i.e. a return to unproductive capital.[17] Further, usury was identified with consumption loans, an illicit return obtained by capitalizing on a neighbour's misfortune. On the other hand, venture capital was productive

---

[16] Miriam Beard, *op. cit.*, pp. 70–1 and 94–5.

[17] As with luxury, the businessmen of Venice and Florence ignored the Church's strictures on usury: 'When we search through the monumental eight volumes of Davidsohn's *History of Florence*, we find mention of one Italian, who objected to taking interest on a loan. He was a rustic nobleman, however; that was back in 1302; and finally he did accept 7 per cent from the banking house of Mozzi. But he preferred another name for it; he felt more comfortable when it was called a "gift" tendered "purely out of love and friendship". . . . In Italy . . . back in the 1300s, the Frescobaldi had charged a king of England no less than 260 per cent.' *Ibid.*, pp. 116–17.

and entitled to a return. As we shall see, the distinction between *rentier* and venture capital or unproductive versus productive capital constantly reappears in the history of economic analysis.

(B) THE MERCANTILISTS

The Transitional Period:

Although we come across the first beginnings of capitalist production as early as the fourteenth or fifteenth century, sporadically, in certain towns of the Mediterranean, the capitalistic era dates from the sixteenth century. Wherever it appears, the abolition of serfdom has been long effected, and the highest development of the middle ages, the existence of sovereign towns, has been long on the wane.[18]

Beer divided English mercantilism into two periods:

(i) from Edward I, or more systematically from Edward III, to Queen Elizabeth; and (ii) from the Stuarts to the ascension of the Hanoverians. The basic idea remained throughout—namely, getting treasure into the realm, but the methods employed for accomplishing that aim and end were different. In the first period, personal monarchy enacted so-called bullionist ordinances and statues for that purpose. In the second period, the merchants attempted to accomplish that aim by the balance of trade policy.[19]

---

[18] Karl Marx, *Capital* (Kerr edition), Vol. I, p. 787. 'Venice was founded, like Liverpool, upon the slave trade. Florence, in the age of Giotto, was already a medieval Manchester, bringing raw materials from afar, making them up by highly complex processes, and distributing them throughout Europe more cheaply than the craftsmen of other places could afford to. . . . As the estates around Florence were absorbed by moneylenders and neighbouring towns were captured and despoiled by military force, the character of rural life was altered to a degree unexampled elsewhere in the Middle Ages. Serfs were "emancipated" and flocked to town as labour proletariat. In the villages a "putting-out system" of spinning was established. . . . [There was a] silk-mill, run by water-power at Bologna, which in 1341, did "the work of 4,000 spinning women," as the old contract with the municipality specifies.' Miriam Beard, *op, cit.*, pp. 126, 133–4.

[19] Beer, *op. cit.*, pp. 61–2. It may seem ambiguous to speak of a first stage of 'mercantilism' in which the interests of the merchants are frequently subordinated to the Crown. However, the taxonomic difficulty vanishes if we interpret Beer's first period as a transitional one, e.g. 'The two hundred-odd years which separated Edward III and Elizabeth were certainly transitional in character. A merchant bourgeoisie had grown to wealth and influence. Having won a measure of privilege, it stood in a position of co-partner rather than antagonist to the nobility, and in Tudor times partly merged with it.' Maurice Dobb, *Studies in the Development of Capitalism*, London, 1946, p. 20.

In the personal monarchy period of mercantilism, Crown policies at first facilitated accumulation; later, however, the policies of the Crown came into contradiction with the requirements for economic growth.

Capital accumulation was facilitated by the strengthening of the Crown *vis à vis* barons, ecclesiastics and foreign princes:

> Money was indispensable to render it possible for the Crown to displace the centrifugal, rebellious baronial and ecclesiastical administrative bodies by creating of non-feudal elements a centralized royal administration and defence force in order to consolidate the Kingdom and secure the royal possessions outside the Kingdom.[20]

A centralized royal administration meant increased court and military expenditures channelled through a bureaucracy and, hence, the centralization of capital; i.e. the tiny accumulations of the cities found their way into the centre of a national economy.[21]

Accumulation was further facilitated by the creation of staple towns, i.e. places designated by the Crown where staple commodities could be sent, weighed and customed for export. But the Crown

> favoured the foreign trader, for he brought treasure either as loans to the Crown or paid in gold and silver inward and outward customs to the Exchequer. The English trader had to struggle hard in order to obtain a part of the foreign trade. He had even to fight for the appointment of Englishmen as customs officials, the Kings preferred foreign 'customers and searchers'. . . . From the point of view of the English merchant, the whole transaction reduced itself to barter, the only beneficiary being the King, who got his customs, subsidies, impositions, etc. . . . The treasure of the trading community did not undergo any change. There was but an exchange of goods of equal value.[22]

[20] Beer, *op. cit.*, p. 63.
[21] 'Among the most powerful influences promoting bourgeois accumulation were the growth of banking institutions and the extension of Crown borrowing and State debt.' Dobb, *op. cit.*, p. 189.
[22] Beer, *op. cit.*, p. 189. 'The staple rights of German towns differed from the English staple in that they were maintained primarily in the interests of the several towns.' Note by W. J. Ashley to Gustav Schmoller's *The Mercantile System* (translated by W. J. Ashley), New York and London, 1896, p. 10, n. 2.

The subordination of the interests of the merchants to the Crown also was evident in the action of Edward IV. In exchange for financial help to equip an expedition to return to England, the Hanseatic League received from Edward in 1474

> unaltered and unimpinged their old privileges without having to concede any rights to the Englishmen in the Baltic towns. They immediately stepped into the place they had occupied in English economic life in the first half of the century, and this place they were to preserve until well into the Tudor era.[23]

The conflict of interest between the Crown and merchants was recognized by John Hales in the middle of the sixteenth century. In a dialogue between a doctor and a knight, the knight replies to the doctor's suggestion that native manufactures should be encouraged:

> Marie, theare you speake a thinge that the Kinges attornie would not agree unto; for if such ware weare made within the Realme, then the kinges custome should be lesse, by reason that little or no such wares should come from beyond the sease.[24]

In the personal monarchy stage of mercantilism, accumulation of treasure was recognized as the appropriate form of capital accumulation; and the development of a national economy greatly stimulated production and trade. Frequently, however, such accumulation was fostered at the expense of domestic manufactures, although—since it was illegal to carry treasure out of the country—there was some encouragement to domestic production. As has been indicated, however, the English trading community did not much increase its stock of treasure. Productive labour was labour that increased the wealth of the Crown; but trade *per se*, both internal and external, was still considered from the medieval point of view of commutative justice. The idea of a favourable balance of trade had not yet taken root.[25] The policy of provision or 'hunger

---

[23] *The Cambridge Economic History of Europe* (edited by M. M. Postan and H. J. Habakkuk), Cambridge, 1952, Vol. II, p. 249.

[24] *A Discourse of the Common Weal of this Realm of England*, 1549 (Lamont edition), pp. 65–6.

[25] This explains the friendly attitude of the early mercantilists toward the work people. 'Thomas Mun . . . never failed to plead in favour of the workman.

for goods', characteristic of medieval towns, remained dominant.[26] Nevertheless, in this transitional period even the policy of provision underwent an evolution. Thus, luxury was still condemned but the rationale changed:

> The hostility towards luxury imports was connected with a similar hostility towards the import of *non-durable* articles which, according to primitive economic notions, were inferior to any durable goods. . . . The import of wine, for instance, was formerly encouraged in every possible way, while later it was the lack of durability of this commodity which made its importation seem indefensible. . . . As early as 1463, a statute complained against the 'inordinate Array and Apparel to the great Displeasure of God, Realms and Countries, to the final Destruction of this said Realm'. Here religious and protectionist considerations were joined in a higher unity. In the following century and a half, until 1604, the legislature in England was very active against every kind of luxury, and the mercantilist point of view made itself felt more and more. In two ordinances of 1574 and 1588, Cecil referred directly to the balance of trade as a cause for anti-luxury measures. Nor was this characteristic of England alone. The introduction of the merchants' *cahier* at the meeting of the French Estates General in 1560 complained of the effect of luxury on morals, and then spoke of 'the large

[26] 'The whole complicated system of regulations as to markets and forestalling is nothing but a skilful contrivance so to regulate supply and demand between the townsman who buys and the countryman who sells, that the former may find himself in as favourable a position as possible, the latter in as unfavourable as possible, in the business of bargaining. . . . The prohibition of the export of grain, wool, and woolfells was among the most usual means for regulating the local market in the local interest; and it constantly led to a complete stoppage of trade. . . . The limitation of the exportation of the currency and of the precious metals frequently occurs in the case of the town as early as the thirteenth century. In intermunicipal commerce we find the first germ of the theory of the balance of trade. It is to be seen in the efforts the towns were constantly making to bring about a direct exchange of wares, and to render this compulsory—as in the Baltic trade—by statutes and ordinances which aimed at preventing the regular flow of the precious metals to foreign countries.' Gustav Schmoller, *The Mercantile System* (translated by W. J. Ashley), New York and London, 1896, pp. 8–10.

He asked the masters, who owned and enjoyed the fruits produced by the craftsmen, to care for the well-being of the work people. He even expected that the taxes on bread should be compensated by a corresponding rise of wages, so that the burden should fall on the rich, "who are either idle, or at least work not in this kind, yet have the use and are great consumers of the poor's labour",' Beer, *op cit.*, p. 177. By 'rich' Mun meant the nobility.

amount of money which left the country in the form of per-
fumery, perfumed gloves, embroidery and so on'.[27]

The Triumph of Mercantilism:

Antonio Serra, a native of Cosenza, formulated 'What is
probably the first systematic statement of the Mercantilist
philosophy'.[28] Serra begins by first pointing out that it is
obvious that gold and silver should abound in a kingdom.[29]
Next he considers the two ways by which gold can be obtained,
viz. natural and collateral means. 'Natural means' refers to
mining; 'collateral means' refers to trade. The collateral means
are relevant and important to 'our kingdom and all of Italy'.
Serra emphasizes the importance of industry over agriculture,
since (1) industry is not dependent upon the weather, (2)
agricultural produce is limited by size of a country's territory
whereas industry is not, (3) trades have a surer market since,
unlike agricultural produce, articles of industry will not spoil
and, hence, can be removed to another place if the market is
poor in one locale, (4) there is more profit from manufacture
than from agriculture. Further, Serra would not prohibit the
export of money. Rather, the export of money makes it possible
for a country to obtain goods that it needs. Also, through the
export of money it is possible for a merchant to transport
goods from one foreign country to another and thus gain the
profit of the carrying trade. Serra would only have prohibited
the export of money in the unlikely case that foreigners held all
the industry of a kingdom in their hands and, further, if there
were nothing left in the kingdom to sell!

Petty, 'the founder of political economy', emphasized the
importance of the accumulation of treasure:

And encrease even of people and Trade, without superlucration,
is not encrease of wealth; nor is superlucration of perishing
commodityes, and such as are triviall or temporary essence the

---

[27] Eli F. Heckscher, *Mercantilism* (translated by Mendel Shapiro), London,
1934, Vol. II, pp. 109–10.

[28] Arthur Eli Monroe, *Early Economic Thought*, Cambridge, Mass., p. 144.
According to Schumpeter, Serra must 'be credited with being the first to compose
a scientific treatise . . . on economic principle and policy'. Joseph A. Schumpeter,
History of Economic Analysis, New York, 1954, p. 195.

[29] *A Brief Treatise On The Causes Which Can Make Gold and Silver Plentiful
In Kingdoms Where There Are No Mines*, 1613, in Monroe, *op. cit.*, pp. 145 ff.

best increase of wealth. But 'tis the superlucration of gold, silver, precious stones, etc., which neither are perishable nor beholding to the change and hurry of times and places for their value, but are morally speaking perpetuall and universall wealth.[30]

Along with the (correct) emphasis on the importance of the accumulation of liquid wealth,[31] the mercantilists stressed the distinction between productive and unproductive labour:

Like Plato, some early English writers considered retailing the least productive of all acquisitive occupations; a single manufacturer, said the author of Britannia Languens, 'adds more in a year to the wealth of the nation than all such retailers and shop-keepers in England'. Grew agreed entirely; indeed he proposed to reduce not only the number of retailers but to eliminate three-fourths of England's ale-house keepers, plus hundreds of pawnbrokers, stock-jobbers, quack doctors and apothecaries, and to reduce drastically the number of lawyers and physicians. John Pollexfen advocated a similar programme, insisting that the government must vigilantly hold the unproductive to a minimum lest otherwise the nation be 'defrauded' of 'so many hands which would be more useful in the mines, or at husbandry, or in the fishing trade or manufactures'. Petty also was deeply concerned about professional redundancy, in fact his plea for enforcing uniform religious worship rested on a fear that dissenting sects would lead to a multiplication of livings and would decrease the number of persons available for productive purposes.[32]

[30] *The Petty Papers* (edited by the Marquis of Lansdowne), London, 1927, Vol. I, p. 214. In view of the above quotation, one cannot accept as correct the following statement by Paul Studenski: 'Smith's introduction of the restricted material production concept . . . can be said to have been a serious interruption in the logical development of economic analysis begun by William Petty and to have retarded the growth of national income theory and practice.' *The Income of Nations*, New York University Press, 1958, p. 19.

[31] It is no argument with the monetary system to say that a ton of iron whose price is £3 constitutes a value of the same magnitude as £3 worth of gold. The point here is not the magnitude of the exchange value, but as to what constitutes its adequate form. If the monetary and mercantile systems single out international trade and the particular branches of national industry directly connected with that trade as the only true sources of wealth or money, it must be borne in mind, that in that period . . . Products, as a rule, were not turned into commodities nor, therefore, into money . . . and did not, in fact, constitute bourgeois wealth.' Karl Marx, *Critique of Political Economy*, Chicago, 1904, pp. 216–17.

[32] E. A. J. Johnson, *Predecessors of Adam Smith*, New York, 1937, p. 245.

13

Assuming that England's population was six millions, Petty estimated the number of productive labourers as 1,800,000. Petty's calculation was based on the following assumptions: (1) two millions of the population were children below the age of seven and, hence, unproductive; (2) of the two million women in the population, one-fourth were engaged in productive labour—baking, brewing, gardening, spinning, lace making, etc.—and 'are equivalent to 500,000 adult workmen'; (3) 500,000 were males between the ages of seven and seventeen —although 'above 100,000 needlessly loose their tymes in learning lattine & greeke. The rest are equivalent to . . . 500,000 adult workmen'; (4) of the remaining 1,500,000, there were 800,000 productive workers—100,000 artisans and 700,000 seamen, husbandmen, handicraftsmen and labourers. The unproductive class consisted of ministers, merchants, soldiers, physicians, lawyers, 'gamesters, cheates, thieves, mercenary whore-bawds, beggars by Trade and Impotents'.[33]

The mercantilist emphasis on the accumulation of liquid wealth through a favourable balance of trade determined the criterion for productive labour. The accumulation bias meant not only the repudiation of a utility theory of value[34] but, also, the condemnation of luxuries. Whereas luxury had been condemned by medieval thinkers as sinful, the mercantilists condemned luxury 'because it tended to weaken England's productive power; because it did not contribute to making England self-sufficient, but tended to increase imports and thereby succor England's competitors. The point of view had now become primarily economic'.[35]

The economic philosophy of the mercantilists constituted a coherent body of thought. Capital accumulation necessitated

[33] *The Petty Papers* (Lansdowne edition), Vol. II, p. 238.
[34] e.g. Francis Bacon wrote: 'The increase of any estate must be upon the foreigner, for whatsoever is somewhere gotten is somewhere lost.' *Essays* XV. Quoted by Beer, *op. cit.*, p. 59.
[35] E. A. J. Johnson, *op. cit.*, pp. 289–90. However, on purely economic grounds the merchants were ambivalent about restraining luxury since (1) sumptuary laws might invite retaliation and (2) the desire for luxury might stimulate national industry. *Ibid.*, pp. 292 ff. Again, 'Most of the large industries set up by Colbert were to make articles of luxury; if France was to sell them abroad, to obtain the steady flow of gold which mercantilists thought necessary, she must become arbiter of fashion. She must set the modes, as well as supply them; it was as important for her to develop cultured taste as to acquire habits of industry; she must become educated as well as busy.' Miriam Beard, *op. cit.*, p. 368.

a favourable balance of trade in which the emphasis on liquid wealth, gold and silver, took precedence. In turn, a favourable balance of trade required a large and poorly paid home population in order to successfully compete in foreign markets. Further, colonies were necessary both as a source of supply for cheap raw materials and as markets for manufactured goods.[36] State intervention, which included the granting of both internal and external monopolies, subsidies and tariffs, legislation against rising wages, etc., was the appropriate method of implementing the programme. The connection between a favourable balance of trade and the concept of productive labour is well summarized in the following:

> We are not concerned with the correctness of the reasoning by which these writers persuaded themselves that increase in national wealth depended upon an increase in the supply of money, but only with tracing the connection between this idea and the doctrine of employment. It is apparent that . . . [mercantilists] . . . believed the source of national wealth to be in the last analysis the labour of the people, that the exploitation of this source demanded a full employment of the working classes, and that increasing stocks of silver and gold would lead to full employment.[37]

Implicit in mercantilist writings is the distinction between productive (venture) and unproductive (*rentier*) capital. True, mercantilists recognized the inevitability of interest. Nevertheless, an abundance of gold and silver would lower the rate of interest and thus stimulate investment.

> How easily the mercantilist mind distinguished between the rate of interest and the marginal efficiency of capital is illustrated by a passage (printed in 1621) which Locke quotes from *A Letter to a Friend concerning Usury*: 'High Interest decays Trade. The advantage from Interest is greater than the Profit from Trade, which makes the rich Merchants give over, and put their Stock to Interest, and the lesser Merchants Break.' Fortrey (*England's Interest and Improvement*, 1663) affords another

[36] The extensive utilization of slave labour was crucial if the colonies were to fulfil their function of providing cheap raw materials. Thus, at the beginning of the nineteenth century, it is estimated that there were seven million slaves in the European colonial districts. Cf. Henryk Grossman, *Das Akkumulations—und Zusammenbruchsgesetz des kapitalistischen Systems*, Leipzig, 1929, p. 413.

[37] Edgar S. Furniss, *The Position of the Labourer in a System of Nationalism* (Kelly & Millman reprint), New York, 1957, p. 66.

example of the stress laid on a low rate of interest as a means of increasing wealth.[38]

(C) THE PHYSIOCRATS

In the sequence of economic analysis, Schumpeter suggests the following analogy: 'Cantillon was to Quesnay, and Petty was to Cantillon, what Ricardo was to Marx.'[39] The roots of the purely economic analysis of the physiocrats are found in Richard Cantillon's thesis that from landed property 'all the inhabitants of the State derive their living and all their wealth'.[40] Here is anticipated the physiocratic tenet that only labour applied in agriculture yields a surplus:

> It is true that the Wool, for example, which is brought from the country, when made up into Cloth in the City is worth four times its former value. But this increase of value, which is the price of the Labour of the Workmen and Manufacturers in the City, is exchanged for the Country produce which serves for their maintenance.[41]

In determining the numbers of productive workers, Cantillon estimated that '25 grown persons suffices to provide 100 others,

[38] J. M. Keynes, *General Theory of Employment, Interest and Money*, p. 344.

[39] *Op. cit.*, p. 218. However, the contribution of Boisguilbert to physiocratic doctrine must not be overlooked. Thus, in the final article of a series, DuPont de Nemours wrote: 'We just now recall a book that it is indeed astonishing that we should have forgotten, as it is one of the first that we have read as we possess two copies of it. This book is *Le Detail de la France*, by M. Pierre le Pesant, Seigneur de Bois-Guilbert. . . . This work . . . is . . . singularly precious on account of the sagacity with which the author understood all that of which the world in his time was ignorant: the necessity to respect the advances of useful labour, and the advantages of liberty of commerce. If he had seen that land and waters were the sole sources from which the labour of man can obtain wealth, and that labour of conservation, of manufacture, of exchange, etc., that have been quite improperly confounded under the generic term of industrial labour, did nothing except to exert itself on wealth already produced without adding anything thereupon; if he had recognized the existence of the net product, and distinguished it from the costs of reproduction; if he had combined these truths with the others that he sensed, the honour of originating the principles of economic science would be due him.' 'Notice abrege,' etc., *Ephemerides du citoyen*. Sept. 1769, pp. 8–10. Quoted by Hazel Van Dyke Roberts, *Boisguilbert: Economist of the Reign of Louis XIV*. New York, 1935, p. 324. For further reference to Boisguilbert, see below, p. 23.

[40] *Essai sur la Nature du Commerce en General* (edited with an English translation by Henry Higgs), London, 1931, p. 57.

[41] *Ibid.*, p. 139.

also grown up, with all the necessaries of life according to the European standard'. The unproductive members of society constitute one-half who 'are either too young or too old for daily work' as well as 'Proprietors of Land, Sick, or Undertakers of different sorts who do not by the Labour of their hands, contribute to the different needs of men'. There remain 25 persons 'who are capable of working but would have nothing to do'. Some of these would be employed as soldiers and domestic servants; however, a country will be rich to the extent that the remaining 25 are employed in the fabrication of durable objects such as houses, furniture, the making of fine linen and cloth, etc.[42]

Cantillon held that only agriculture was productive (surplus yielding); nevertheless, he believed that a society increases in wealth to the extent that the unproductive members fix their labour in durable commodities. Like Petty before him, Cantillon deplored clerical redundancy:

Experience shows that the Countries which have embraced Protestantism and have neither Monks nor Mendicants have become visibly more powerful. They have also the advantage of having suppressed a great number of Holy Days when no work is done in Roman Catholic countries, and which diminish the labour of the People by about an eighth part of the year.[43]

Concerning the accumulation of durable commodities, the increase of gold and silver through mining and foreign trade will most enrich a nation:

. . . Metals are not only durable but so to speak permanent, which fire itself cannot destroy, which are generally accepted as the Measure of Value, and which can always be exchanged for any of the necessities of life.[44]

In his discussion of the circulation of money, Cantillon also anticipated Quesnay's *Tableau Economique*:

The circulation of this money takes place when the Landlords spend in detail in the City the rents which the Farmers have paid them in lump sums, and when the Undertakers of the Cities, Butchers, Bakers, Brewers, etc. collect little by little this

---

[42] *Ibid.*, p. 87. [43] *Ibid.*, p. 95.

[44] *Ibid.*, p. 89. In the event that useful employment cannot be found for all members of the unproductive class, Cantillon sees 'no objection to encouraging employment which serves only for ornament or amusement'. (p. 91).

same money to buy from the Farmers in lump sums Cattle, Wheat, Barley, etc. In this way all the large sums of money are distributed in small amounts, and all the small amounts are then collected to make payments in large amounts, directly or indirectly, to the Farmers, and this money large or small always passes in return for services.[45]

It will not do, however, to see in Cantillon a philosopher of the 'natural order'. Rather, Cantillon's economics reflect the transitional period in which he lived. Clear as to the mechanics of foreign trade (the price–specie–flow mechanism), Cantillon nevertheless supported state policies to increase the import of treasure. The home country should encourage the export of manufactured goods in exchange for specie, which constitute 'the best returns or payments'.

According to Cantillon, a country that achieves an increase in specie from a favourable balance of trade is far better off than one in which the increased specie results from the discovery of gold and silver mines, e.g. Spain and Portugal. In the former case, increased specie will create additional employment for merchants, undertakers, mechanics, and workmen 'who furnish the commodities sent to the foreigner from whom the money is drawn'. In the latter case, the increased specie from mining finds its way into foreign countries to pay for imports.[46]

True, the increased specie arising from a favourable balance of trade will lead to a rise in prices and rents.[47] Foreigners will buy elsewhere, as will the landlords of the home country: 'The Wealth acquired by a State through Trade, Labour and Oeconomy will plunge gradually into luxury. States who rise by trade do not fail to sink afterwards.' Be that as it may, Cantillon concluded, 'it is always true that when the State is in actual possession of a Balance of Trade and abundant money it seems powerful, and it is so in reality so long as this abundance continues'.[48]

In population doctrine (demand for labour governs supply),

---

[45] *Ibid.*, pp. 126–7.   [46] *Ibid.*, pp. 159 ff.
[47] But note the qualification '. . . I conclude that by doubling the quantity of money in a State the prices of products and merchandise are not always doubled. A River which runs and winds about in its bed will not flow with double the speed when the amount of its water is doubled.' *Ibid.*, p. 177.
[48] *Ibid.*, pp. 233–7.

18

in the analysis of internal circulation, in the analysis of foreign trade, in the emphasis on internal production (agriculture and the accumulation of durable commodities), in all these Cantillon was ahead or at least abreast of his times. Nevertheless, Cantillon's adherence to a favourable balance of trade doctrine stamps him as a mercantilist. The transition from gains by alienation to gains from production is still incomplete.

Complete repudiation of mercantilist economic philosophy was reserved for Quesnay. Paradoxically, however, Quesnay's liberation was achieved through a desire to reinstate a medieval society in which commutative justice prevailed:

> All the difficulties and incongruities met with in the study of physiocracy would be removed if we considered it as an attempt to rationalize medieval economic life in the light of the progress of philosophy and physical science since the sixteenth century. Quesnay . . . looked back to medieval society and found it ethically more firmly based than modern society. But he also found that all medieval regulations . . . to secure commutative justice or equality of exchanges had failed of their purpose. . . . He had also learned from the physical interpretation of the law of nature that self-interest could not be suppressed. . . . It was therefore best to allow nature and right reason to work in liberty, to remove all those commercial regulations which give to one of the parties an advantage over the other.[49]

Quesnay's feudal bias, however, did not imply a rejection of economic progress. On the contrary, the physiocrats envisioned the establishment of large-scale capitalist agriculture, efficiently organized to maximize a surplus:

> For the Physiocrats, the fundamental problem set by the 'economical structure' of their time was how to increase the national income of an under-developed country like France from a low level to a high one.[50]

In the *Tableau Economique*, Quesnay analysed the circular flow of goods and money in a stationary state. Quesnay assumed three classes, viz. the productive class consisting of capitalists and workers engaged in agriculture, the sterile class consisting of all those engaged in manufacturing and also including merchants, and the landlord class consisting not only

[49] M. Beer, *An Enquiry into Physiocracy*, London, 1939, pp. 147–8.
[50] Ronald L. Meek, *The Economics of Physiocracy*, London, 1962, p. 368.

of landed proprietors 'but also any who have the slightest title to sovereignity of any kind—a survival of feudalism, where the two ideas of sovereignity and property are always linked together'.[51]

Only the agricultural class is productive since only agricultural activity gives rise to a surplus or net product, i.e. output exceeds input. Industrial workers neither create nor destroy value. They merely replace one form of value by another, i.e. the value of their subsistence and the raw material used in production reappears in the value of manufactured goods.[52] The landlords consume the surplus realized from agriculture, the net product. It is assumed that the landlords are entitled to the surplus because either they or their ancestors cleared and drained the land.[53]

In the *Tableau Economique*, Quesnay depicts the process of circulation among the three classes only; he ignores intra-class flows. The starting point is the year's harvest of agricultural produce, which is in the hands of the productive class. This amounts to 5 milliards. Also, Quesnay assumes the productive class to have on hand money to the amount of 2 milliards. From the gross produce of 5 milliards, it is necessary to subtract 2 milliards to replace circulating capital used up in the period of production. Hence only 3 milliards of agricultural produce circulates. Of these 3 milliards, 2 represent the net produce that the landlord class receives as rent; i.e. rent is not considered a cost. The other milliard, however, which enters circulation constitutes the interest on the fixed and circulating capital advanced by capitalist farmers because interest is a necessary cost and therefore enters into the supply price.

The following table presents an extremely simplified version of the physiocratic model of circulation:

[51] Charles Gide and Charles Rist, *A History of Economic Doctrines* (translated by R. Richards) second edition, London (no date), p. 19.

[52] 'This essential difference which the Physiocrats sought to establish between agricultural and industrial production was at bottom theological. The fruits of the earth are given by God, while the products of the arts are wrought by man, who is powerless to create.' *Ibid.*, p. 15.

[53] A further justification for rent is found in private property: 'It is impossible not to recognize the right of property as a divine institution, for it has been ordained that this should be the indirect means of perpetuating the work of creation.' Mercier de la Riviere, *L'Ordre naturel et essential des Societes politiques*, quoted in Gide and Rist, *op. cit.*, p. 21, n. 2.

Steps in Circulation	The Productive Class				The Sterile Class				The Landlord Class		
	Food	Raw Mat.	Mfg. Gds.	Money	Food	Raw Mat.	Mfg. Gds.	Money	Food	Mfg. Gds.	Money
Inventory Prior to Circulation	2	1	0	2	0	0	2	0	0	0	0
1. Productive class pays 2 rent to landlords				−2							2
2. Landlords buy 1 of food from productive class	−1			1					1		−1
3. Landlords buy 1 of mfg. gds. from the sterile class							−1	1		1	−1
4. Productive class buys 1 of mfg. gds. from sterile class			1	−1			−1	1			
5. Sterile class buys 1 of food & 1 of raw mat. from productive class	−1	−1		2	1	1		−2			
Inventory following completion of circular flow	0	0	1	2	1	1	0	0	1	1	0

With the completion of circulation, the productive class is in a position to proceed again with the process of agricultural production. In fact, this simplified model of circulation brings out all the essentials of the physiocratic analysis: (1) the productive class has regained its two milliards of money it advanced and hence both circulation and production can proceed in the next period without interruption (it will be recalled that 2 milliards of circulating capital were withheld from circulation by the productive class); (2) the productive class has received interest in the form of one milliard of manufactured goods; (3) the value of the manufactured goods held by the sterile class at the beginning of circulation has been exchanged for an equal value of raw materials and subsistence;[54] (4) the landlord class has consumed the net product; (5) the model also indicates how the system would be disrupted if the landlords should decide to hoard all or part of the 2 milliards of rent;[55] (6) implicit in the circulation model is a plea for *laissez faire* since government interference could upset the circular flow; (7) similarly, the physiocratic doctrine of a single tax on land finds its justification in the circular flow model; i.e. since both the productive and sterile classes receive only the irreducible minimum necessary to ensure continued production, any tax must finally be paid out of the net product.[56] If then a tax is

[54] Actually, since the entrepreneurs in the sterile class would receive an average rate of profit, the output of the sterile class would be sold above value. Cf. Ronald L. Meek, 'The Physiocratic Concept of Profit', *Economica*, February, 1959, pp. 46 ff.

[55] 'It is necessary that the sum total of the revenue should enter into the annual circulation, and pervade it in its utmost extent; that no pecuniary fortunes be formed, or, at least, there be a compensation between those that are formed, and those which, from extravagance, return into the circulation; for, otherwise, the amassing of pecuniary fortunes would impede the distribution of a part of the annual revenue of the nation, and hold back part of the circulation of the nation, to the prejudice of the advances necessary for the conduct of agriculture, of the recompence of the salary of the artisans, and of the consumption incident to the different classes of men who exercise lucrative professions: and this reduction would inevitably diminish the revenue reproduced.' Quesnay, *Maximes Générales du Gouvernement Economique.* Translated and quoted by the Earl of Lauderdale in *An Inquiry into the Nature and Origin of Public Wealth and into the Means and Causes of its Increase*, London, 1804, pp. 247–8.

[56] According to Quesnay, 'The level of wages and consequently the level of satisfaction which wage workers can receive, are fixed at and reduced to the minimum by extreme competition which never ceases among them. If, then, in some land it will be attempted to force these labourers to reduce in half the sum of their satisfactions by means of taxation, then, they will emigrate to other

levied on either the productive or sterile class it can only result
in impeding circulation and finally production.

The strategic role of agriculture in the physiocratic analysis
gave rise to the concept of *le bon prix*: i.e. the price of agricultural produce must be sufficient to call forth an adequate
supply. *Le bon prix* was originated by Boisguilbert, a contemporary of Colbert, who opposed Colbert's mercantilist
policies.

In order to subsidize industry, Colbert had prohibited the
export of agricultural produce, thus depressing its price. In
this way, industry could pay a lower subsistence wage to its
workers and hence compete more favourably in foreign markets.
Boisguilbert argued that this policy was mistaken since '. . .
causing the entrepreneurs to lose, they cease their traffic
entirely, which causes a high payment (*qui fait payer la falle
enchere*) for the preceding abasement of the product'.[57] Hence,
Boisguilbert pleaded for a system of *laissez faire*.[58] Similarly,
Quesnay desired to repeal the laws prohibiting the export of
grain:

> . . . the entire edifice of agricultural prosperity rests in the last
> analysis on the 'good price' (*le bon prix*). The price of grains
> and other agricultural produce must be considerably in excess
> of their cost of production. Therefore domestic consumption
> by both the rich and the poor must be stimulated; tolls and

[57] *Traite des grains*, p. 589. Quoted by Hazel Van Dyke Roberts, *op. cit.*,
p. 269.

[58] However, as Roberts points out, Boisguilbert qualified the doctrine with
respect to agriculture. What Boisguilbert wanted was 'proportional prices' or,
in modern terms, parity for agriculture. That is, Boisguilbert believed agricultural prices were flexible; whereas, non-agricultural prices were inflexible downward. Therefore, Boisguilbert recommended that government should encourage
the export of grain in periods of abundance and prohibit its export in times of
scarcity. According to Roberts, this qualification by Boisguilbert did not constitute a theoretical denial of *laissez faire* but rather a realistic appraisal of the
improbability of achieving *laissez faire* during his time. *Ibid.*, pp. 249 ff.

countries where their existence is more secure and their labour better protected.
Then the small number of those who remain . . . will dictate their conditions to
the employers, and force them to pay normal wages as well as the tax and the
expenses of cultivating the soil. Therefore, these original owners of land, being
tied to the land by their ownership of it, must necessarily bear the brunt of such
destructive taxation.' 'Second probleme economique' (1767) translated and
quoted by Michael T. Wermel in *The Evolution of the Classical Wage Theory*,
New York, 1939, pp. 58–9.

local prohibitions on traffic in agricultural commodities must be abolished; an equalization of market prices between provinces and from year to year, which is advantageous to the producers and detrimental solely to middlemen, must be insured by free competition. . . . The export of agricultural commodities should at all times be perfectly free; even if the quantity exported is very small the domestic producers will benefit by the opportunity to sell at the price prevailing in the world market. . . . Finally, no unfair protection against the legitimate competition of foreign producers must be allowed to industry and active competition must be fostered among domestic manufactures, in order that the prices of industrial products be forced down to the fairest level.[59]

In the *General Maxims*, Quesnay emphasized that the 'good price' for agricultural produce was advantageous to the poorer classes:

> *That it should not be believed that cheapness of produce is profitable to the lower classes;* for a low price of produce causes a fall in the wages of the lower orders of people, reduces their well-being, makes less work and remunerative occupations available for them, and destroys the nation's revenue.

A fall in wages is inimical to the national interest because of the decline in effective demand:

> *That the well-being of the latter classes of citizens should not be reduced;* for then they would not be able to contribute sufficiently to the consumption of the produce which can be consumed only within the country, which would bring about a reduction in the reproduction and revenue of the nation.[60]

Although the physiocrats held that the merchant–manufacturing class was sterile, they recognized that some members of this class were useful and necessary:

> . . . the artisans, craftsmen, professional men, merchants, and traffickers are an unproductive (sterile) class. Some sections of this class are doing useful social work, and hence deserve a remuneration, a salary for their labour and expense, while other sections, particularly the traffickers and the redundant trades-

---

[59] G. Weulersse, 'The Physiocrats', in 'Economics', *Encyclopedia of Social Sciences*, Vol. V, p. 350.
[60] Quesnay, *General Maxims*, XIX and XX, Ronald L. Meek, *op. cit.*, p. 236.

people, are injurious to the welfare of the community, for it is evident that their income, which is often relatively large, is a deduction from, and diminution of, the income of the productive class, thus crippling it in the cultivation of the soil, that is, in the production of riches.[61]

The sterile class rendered a service to the productive class by furnishing manufactured goods that aided agricultural production. Further, the sterile class provided a market for surplus agricultural produce. Similarly, as has been indicated, foreign trade although unproductive could confer benefits, e.g. by importing useful commodities that were produced more cheaply abroad. Again, foreign trade could provide an outlet for any home surplus of agricultural produce:

> In a natural order, that is where trade is unrestricted, the exchanges are always equal, and both countries benefit by mutually supplying their deficiencies. In such cases the interest of agriculture and commerce or between merchants and the nation are in harmony. . . . Where, however, merchants turn into traffickers (*marchands revendeurs*), then their interests and those of the nation are diametrically opposed.
>
> Traffic is buying, transporting, selling, importing and exporting, re-importing and re-exporting any goods which offer anywhere a chance for profit—a ceaseless process of purchases and sales, which accumulates fruitless expenses and gives rise to the expectation of salaries, which the productive classes of the nation have to meet.[62]

Because trade gave rise to 'fruitless expenses', the physiocrats qualified their *laissez faire* doctrine with respect to interest. Government should set a legal maximum rate, and this maximum rate 'should be the revenue drawn from a piece of land, the value which equals the loan money',[63] i.e. the lender should receive a return equal to the amount he would have obtained if instead of loaning his money he had purchased land.

Luxury expenditures would also dissipate the surplus and thus retard investment in agriculture:

> *That no encouragement at all should be given to luxury in the*

[61] M. Beer, *An Enquiry into Physiocracy*, pp. 122–3.
[62] *Ibid.*, pp. 129–30.
[63] *Ibid.*, p. 138.

way of ornamentation to the detriment of the expenditure involved in the operations and improvement of agriculture, and of the expenditure on the consumption of subsistence goods, which sustains the market for raw produce, its proper price, and the reproduction of the nation's revenue.[64]

Excessive government expenditures also 'could swallow up all the wealth of the nation and sovereign'. However, excessive economizing is not desirable since many government expenditures facilitate agricultural production,[65] e.g. improvements of roads and rivers.

Most important, the physiocrats stressed the antithesis between productive and unproductive (*rentier*) capital.

That the state should avoid contracting loans which create rentier incomes, which burden it with devouring debts, and which bring about a trade or traffic in finance, through the medium of negotiable bills, the discount of which causes a greater and greater increase in sterile monetary fortunes. These fortunes separate finance from agriculture, and deprive the countryside of the wealth necessary for the improvement of landed property and for the operations involved in the cultivation of the land.[66]

In short, finance capital is not only a cost to the economy but through the formation of 'sterile monetary fortunes' (hoarding) disrupts the circular flow, i.e. reduces effective demand.

The medieval bias of the physiocratic school meant the repudiation of mercantilism, which was incompatible with commutative justice. But whereas in medieval doctrine the merchant who transports commodities performs productive labour, in the physiocratic doctrine all trading is unproductive. The essential difference in the analysis of trade stems from divergent theories of value. Since medieval writers adopted a

---

[64] Quesnay, *General Maxims* XXII, Ronald L. Meek, *op. cit.*, p. 326. 'But not all expenditure on luxury goods constitutes luxury. It is necessary to make a clear distinction between conspicuous consumption (*faste*) and luxury (*luxe*). *Luxe* is very often *faste*, but *faste* is not necessarily *luxe*. . . . Conspicuous consumption, in other words, is not luxury when it does not detrimentally affect the capitalization of agriculture.' Ronald Meek, 'Early Theories of Under-Consumption', *The Economics of Physiocracy*, p. 317. Meek further points out certain types of conspicuous consumption were preferable to others. *Ibid.*, pp. 317–18.

[65] Quesnay, *General Maxims* XXVII in Meek, *op. cit.*, p. 237.

[66] *Ibid.*, p. 238.

utility theory of value, it followed that the service of the trader (place utility) was productive. But since for the physiocrats only agriculture was productive, the trader, at best, could only perform useful services.

The contradictions within physiocracy have been well summarized by Marx:

> The physiocratic system is indeed the first system which contains an analysis of capitalistic production. . . . Feudalism . . . is portrayed and interpreted *sub specie* of bourgeois production, and agriculture appears as that branch of production in which capitalistic production—the production of surplus value—can exclusively be found. Feudalism thus acquires bourgeois characteristics, and in the process the bourgeois society acquires a feudal appearance. . . . The apparent glorification of landed property turns into its economic negation and into capitalistic production. . . . The burden of taxation is in its entirety placed on land rent because land rent is the only surplus value. . . . With taxation placed exclusively on landed property, industry becomes exempt from taxation and, thereby, from all government intervention. This is allegedly done in the interest of the landed property, not in that of industry. . . . One can understand how the feudal appearance of the physiocratic system, similar to the aristocratic garb of the enlightenment, turned the masses of feudal lords into sentimental followers and propagandists of a system which in its substance proclaimed the establishment of the bourgeois system of production on the ruins of feudalism.[67]

The physiocratic tenet that only agriculture was productive explains the relatively brief historical popularity of the school. Obviously, such a doctrine could not provide the rationale for bourgeois accumulation. Yet the physiocratic emphasis on gains from production rather than trade constituted an advance in economic theorizing. The genius of the school consisted in its recognition of the fundamental problem of a market economy, viz. the necessity not only to maximize an economic surplus but also to secure an adequate market for production. The physiocrats saw both the cost side and the market side of production.

[67] Karl Marx, *Theorien uber den Mehrwert* in *The Development of Economic Thought* (edited and translated by Henry William Spiegel), New York, 1952, pp. 107-9.

II

THE CLASSICAL ECONOMISTS

WE HAVE SEEN that it was not until the development of mercantilism that it became possible to differentiate activities strictly according to their 'productiveness', i.e. their contribution to accumulation. Similarly, the theory of the net product enabled the physiocrats to distinguish sharply between productive (surplus-yielding) and non-productive activities.

However, given a utility theory of value, it is impossible to effectively conceptualize a distinction between productive and unproductive labour. True, medieval writers distinguished between 'proper' commerce and speculative or usurious transactions, but the distinction was grounded in ethics rather than economics. Proper commerce yielded place utility; only speculative and usurious activities could be regarded as 'unproductive' in that there was no commensurate *quid pro quo*. The history of the attenuation of the usury doctrine or, better, the metamorphosis of usury into immoderate interest attests to the impossibility of the distinction:

> What is left of the usury rule, merged as it now is in practice with the demand for a just price, is an objection to immoderate interest. It would be perhaps impossible to think of a transaction involving the extension of credit at a moderate profit which could not have been justified in terms of the revised scholastic analysis.[1]

Similarly, in time, speculation is accepted. Speculators balance supply and demand, thus reducing price fluctuations and also enabling producers to hedge. In short, subject to certain institutional restraints, a utility theory of value equally legitimates all phenomena of a free market.

[1] Noonan, *op. cit.*, pp. 361–2.

28

The Classical Economists

With the exception of the physiocrats, the forerunners of economic liberalism proceeded on the basis of a utility theory of value. That is to say, to the extent that value theorizing can be deduced or imputed, the orientation was utilitarian. For example, in defending free trade, Dudley North wrote:

> Trade is nothing else but a commutation of Superfluities; for instance: I give of mine, what I can spare, for somewhat of yours, which I want, and you can spare.[2]

Similarly, the anonymous author in *Considerations on the East India Trade* (1701) who attacked monopolies and restrictions on the export of bullion and who emphasized the advantages of the division of labour, of inventions and of external economies resulting from population concentration, justified free trade on the grounds that money sent abroad can purchase a greater quantity of goods than at home. Again, the emphasis is utilitarian:

> ... The true and principal Riches, whether of private Persons, or of whole Nations, are Meat, and Bread, and Cloaths, and Houses, and Conveniences as well as Necessaries of Life; the several Refinements and Improvements of these, the secure Possession and Enjoyment of them. ... For, why are we surrounded with the Sea? Surely that our Wants at home might be supply'd by our Navigation into other Countries, the least and easiest labour. By this we taste the Spices of Arabia, yet never feel the scorching Sun which brings them forth; we shine in Silks which our Hands have never wrought; we drink of Vineyards which we never planted; the Treasures of those Mines are ours, in which we have never digged; we only plough the Deep, and reap the Harvest of every Country in the World.[3]

In the Fable of the Bees, Mandeville provided a utilitarian rationale:

---

[2] Dudley North, *Discourses Upon Trade* (1691) in *Early English Tracts on Commerce*, edited by J. R. McCulloch (Cambridge, England, 1954 reprint), p. 516. North anticipated Mandeville (see below) when he wrote: 'The main spur to Trade ... is the exorbitant Appetites of Men, which they will take pains to gratifie, and so be disposed to work, when nothing else will incline them to it; for did Men content themselves with bare necessities, we should have a poor World.' *Ibid.*, p. 528.

[3] *Early English Tracts on Commerce*, pp. 558 and 585.

Thus Vice nurs'd Ingenuity,
Which join'd with Time and Industry
Had carry'd Life's Conveniencies,
Its real Pleasures, Comforts, Ease
To such a Height, the very Poor
Liv'd better than the Rich before
And nothing could be added more.[4]

Kenneth Burke provides an excellent summary of Mandeville's contribution to economic liberalism:

The new economic structure has, by this time, revealed its outlines with sufficient clarity to necessitate a new code of morals —and Mandeville's fable radically reverses the Church's attitude toward a key value, personal ambition. In the Church's moral scheme, ambition had been a major vice. Mandeville playfully speculated upon the possibility of enshrining it as the major virtue. He fabulously suggested that if people were greedy and pushing enough in personal enterprise, they would produce an abundance of commodities whereby the whole community would profit.

In the spirit of high comedy, Mandeville dealt with the same shift in values that Shakespeare had considered tragically in *Macbeth*. Macbeth is the poetic adumbration of the 'Faustian man', who would fulfil his destiny at all costs. He stands at the turning point between the feudal attitude towards ambition, as *punishable pride*, and the commercial attitude towards ambition, as the *essence of vocation*. Shakespeare heralds the new, while fearing it in terms of the old. In Mandeville the conflict is considered less drastically, though he still draws upon it for his literary effects.

By the time we get to Adam Smith, the new code has gained sufficient authority to be framed as *orthodoxy*. Smith proceeds simply by rationalizing Mandeville *without* the paradox; ambition becomes a private virtue because it is a public virtue. The utilitarians completed his theory.[5]

We have seen that with the exception of the physiocrats, the repudiation of mercantilist policies was sanctioned by a utilitarian theory of value. But the utilitarian bias precludes a

[4] Bernard Mandeville, *The Fable of the Bees, or Private Vices, Publick Virtues*, edited by F. B. Kaye (London, 1957 reprint), Vol. I, p. 26. The first edition of Mandeville's work in 1714 passed almost unnoticed. The second edition (1723), almost double the size of the first, was widely read and discussed.

[5] Kenneth Burke, *Attitudes Toward History*, Hermes Publications, Los Altos California, 1959, pp. 23–4.

distinction between productive and unproductive activities. The effect is to ignore or minimize the accumulation problem. Here we have a curious historical parallel: Economic liberalism of the late seventeenth and early eighteenth centuries found its rationale in utilitarianism. Similarly, Neoclassical economics, developed in the last quarter of the nineteenth century, adopted a utilitarian point of view. In both cases, accumulation ceases to be the focal point of economic analysis.

The utilitarian or welfare bias of Neoclassical economics, originating in the late nineteenth century, stresses rational allocation of given resources in contrast to the classical economists' emphasis on increased welfare through accumulation:

> . . . the principal welfare objective of classical economics is to attain a continuous state of economic expansion, rather than to 'tighten' up the equilibrium allocation of resources within a given Static framework. This of course follows from the view that the welfare of society . . . may be regarded as roughly proportional to the volume of output and economic activity. The allocative approach accepts given labour supply, capital equipment and technique as data and tries to make the best of them to satisfy given consumers' preferences.[6]

It was Adam Smith's particular contribution to reconcile the needs of bourgeois accumulation with utilitarianism. Paradoxically, however, this reconciliation required the formulation of a labour theory of value, rather than a utility theory of economic worth. The synthesis was achieved by broadening the physiocratic concept of surplus-yielding activity. All labour that exchanges with capital (as distinct from revenue) is productive. Further, in the process of accumulation, productive labour fixes itself in a vendible commodity, that is, a durable source of utilities. Thus, the wealth of nations is augmented by the production of commodities yielding a stream of services through time, rather than by activities in which production and consumption occur simultaneously.[7]

[6] Hla Myint, *Theories of Welfare Economics*, London School of Economics and Political Science, 1948, p. 87.

[7] In Bentham's *felicific calculus*, duration was one of the dimensions of pleasure. Jeremy Bentham, 1748–1832 (a contemporary of Smith, intimately associated with David Ricardo and James and John Stuart Mill), accepted the classical distinction between productive and unproductive labour. Bentham

Labour provides the surplus for accumulation. In turn, accumulation increases the productive power of labour. The consequent cheapening of commodities means the multiplication of use-values. Thus, there is no conflict between accumulation and utilitarianism:

> Consumption is the sole end and purpose of all production; and the interest of the producer ought to be attended to, only so far as it may be necessary for promoting that of the consumer. The maxim is so perfectly self-evident, that it would be absurd to attempt to prove it.[8]

Similarly, through the market mechanism, Smith follows Mandeville in finding a utilitarian justification for egoism:

> It is not from the benevolence of the butcher, the brewer, or the baker, that we expect our dinner, but from their regard to their own interest. We address ourselves, not to their humanity but to their self-love, and never talk to them of our own necessities but of their advantage.[9]

Since all labour that exchanges with capital is productive, it followed for Smith that the more labour a particular capital puts 'into motion', the greater its productivity:

> Equal capitals . . . will immediately put into motion very different quantities of productive labour, and augment too in very different proportions the value of the annual produce of the land and labour of the society to which they belong.[10]

[8] Adam Smith, *The Wealth of Nations*, Modern Library Reprint of the Edwin Cannan edition (New York, 1937), p. 625.

[9] *Ibid.*, p. 14. For further discussion of the influence of Mandeville on Adam Smith see Cannan's introduction, pp. li–liv. Cf. also F. B. Kaye's introduction to the *Fable of the Bees, op. cit.*, Vol. I, pp. cxvi–cxix, and cxl ff.

[10] Smith, *op. cit.*, p. 343.

recognized that his utilitarian doctrine, 'the greatest happiness of the greatest number', in which pleasure is synonymous with happiness, meant that happiness would be increased by the equalization of income. However, this *obstacle* to accumulation was surmounted by Bentham's dictum that security of income takes precedence over equality of income. As Wesley C. Mitchell put it: 'Unless . . . people had security in the possession of that which they produce; the motive for production would fall away. . . . Indeed, it is doubtful whether men would be left even with subsistence.' Wesley C. Mitchell, *Lecture Notes on Types of Economic Theory* (New York, 1949), Vol. I, pp. 108–9. In his *Defence of Usury* (London, 1787, p. 102) Bentham wrote: 'Those who have resolution to sacrifice the present to the future are natural objects of envy to those who have sacrificed the future to the present. The children who have eaten their cake are natural enemies of the children who have theirs.'

Smith's criterion of capital productivity is value added, i.e. the amount by which the *gross revenue* of society is augmented. Thus, given an average rate of profit, the more labour employed, the greater the value added.

Smith's criterion of value added enabled him to establish a hierarchy of productive capitals. Capital employed in agriculture puts into motion the greatest quantity of productive labour (including 'labouring cattle'). Also, the value added in agriculture is greater since it consists not only of wages and profits but also includes rent.[11] The next most productive capital is that invested in manufacturing, which sets in motion a greater quantity of labour than capital invested in wholesale trade. Within a country, the least productive capital is that of the retailer:

> The capital of the retailer replaces, together with its profits, that of the merchant of whom he purchases goods, and thereby enables him to continue his business. The retailer himself is the only productive labourer whom it immediately employs. In his profits, consists the whole value which its employment adds to the annual produce of the land and labour of the society.[12]

Nevertheless, the retailer performs a valuable service since 'If there was no such trade as a butcher, for example, every man would be obliged to purchase a whole ox or sheep at a time.' Further, the retailer economizes the capital of a 'poor workman' who otherwise would have to tie up much of his capital in means of subsistence. Smith also took issue with those mercantilist writers who were concerned with redundance in retail trade:

> The prejudices of some political writers against shopkeepers and tradesmen, are altogether without foundation . . . they can never be multiplied so as to hurt the publick, though they may

[11] Smith's emphasis on the productivity of agriculture followed from his value-added concept. However, Smith's preoccupation with agriculture might also be attributed to one or more of the following: (1) the influence of the physiocrats for whom Smith had a high regard; (2) the impact of the Agricultural Revolution (Smith wrote prior to the great changes wrought by the Industrial Revolution); (3) Smith's period-of-production analysis in which the wages fund accumulated in a preceding period (consisting primarily of agricultural produce) is available for the maintenance of productive labour in the succeeding period.

[12] *Ibid.*, p. 343. Smith overlooks the wages of the retailer. Elsewhere, however, Smith warns against confounding wages with profits (p. 53).

so as to hurt one another. The quantity of grocery goods, for example, which can be sold in a particular town, is limited by the demand of that town and its neighbourhood. . . . It is not the multitude of ale-houses, to give the most suspicious example, that occasions a general disposition to drunkenness among the common people; but that disposition arising from other causes necessarily gives employment to a multitude of ale-houses.[13]

Whereas capital employed in the wholesale trade within a country 'generally replaces by every such operation two distinct capitals'; capital employed in the foreign trade, 'which sends British goods to Portugal, and brings back Portuguese goods to Great Britain, replaces by every such operation only one British capital'. Further, Smith was of the opinion that capitals employed in foreign trade had a much slower rate of turnover: 'A capital, therefore, employed in the home trade will sometimes make twelve operations . . . before a capital employed in the foreign trade has made one.'[14] Capital employed in the carrying trade is least productive of all, it 'is altogether withdrawn from supporting the productive labour of that particular country, to support that of some foreign countries'.[15]

Because Smith's emphasis was on *gross revenue* (somewhat similar to 'national income' in contemporary usage) his distinction between the productivity of capitals employed at home and abroad is comparable to modern national income analysis. That is, Smith was aware also of income (employment) leakages arising from foreign trade. However, because Smith assumed, given competition, full employment (what is annually saved is annually consumed), such leakages could only occur as the result of wretched mercantilist policies.

In the preceding paragraph we noted that Smith's 'gross revenue' concept was similar to the contemporary 'national income' concept. However, there is an important distinction between these two concepts that requires emphasis. For Smith, income arising out of an exchange of labour with revenue,

[13] *Ibid.*, p. 342.
[14] In a footnote to this passage, Cannan remarks: 'If this doctrine as to the advantage of quick returns had been applied earlier in the chapter, it would have made havoc of the argument as to the superiority of agriculture.' *Ibid.*, p. 349.
[15] *Ibid.*, p. 351.

rather than capital, did not augment gross revenue. Since no value was added, the transaction constituted merely a transfer payment:[16]

> ... the labour of a manufacturer adds, generally, to the value of the materials which he works upon, that of his own maintenance, and of his master's profit. The labour of a menial servant, on the contrary, adds to the value of nothing. Though the manufacturer has his wages advanced to him by his master, he in reality, costs him no expence, the value of those wages being generally restored, together with a profit, in the improved value of the subject upon which his labour is bestowed. But the maintenance of a menial servant . . . does not fix or realize itself in any particular subject or vendible commodity. His services generally perish in the very instant of their performance, and seldom leave any trace or value behind them, for which an equal quantity of service could afterwards be procured.
>
> The labour of some of the most respectable orders in the society is, like that of menial servants, unproductive of any value and does not fix or realize itself in any permanent subject, or vendible commodity. . . . The sovereign . . . all the officers both of justice and war . . . the whole army and navy, are unproductive labourers. . . . Both productive and unproductive labourers, and those who do not labour at all, are all equally maintained by the annual produce of the land and labour of the country. . . . According, therefore, as a smaller or greater proportion of it is in any one year employed in maintaining unproductive hands, the more in the one case and the less in the other will remain for the productive, and the next year's produce will be greater or smaller accordingly; the whole annual produce, if we except the spontaneous productions of the earth, being the effect of productive labour.[17]

Smith emphasized the value-added criterion which, he believed, was synonymous with his durable–vendible–commodity criterion of productive labour. But Smith was inconsistent. Thus, in his polemic with the physiocrats, Smith pointed out that the physiocrats admit the sterile class replaces 'the value of its own annual consumption, and continues, at least, the

---

[16] In modern national income accounting 'transfer payments' refer to those payments that are not a reward for current production, e.g., unemployment relief payments, pensions, business taxes, etc.

[17] Smith, *op. cit.*, pp. 314–15.

stock of capital which maintains and employs it'. Here, the criterion changes from value-added to simple replacement.[18]

Smith's bias towards the accumulation of durable vendible commodities also led the canny Scotsman to distinguish between less and more 'productive' unproductive expenditures. An individual may spend his revenue 'either in things which are consumed immediately . . . or it may be spent in things more durable, which can therefore be accumulated, and in which every day's expense may . . . either alleviate or support and heighten the effect of that of the following day.[19]

The mercantilists had identified the increase of wealth of the merchant class with that of the nation—hence, the mercantilist doctrine of the economy of low wages. With Smith, however, economic progress consisted in the augmentation of gross revenue. The gross revenue concept is clearly utilitarian. A nation prospers and progresses to the extent that all or the majority of its citizens prosper. This follows for Smith because saving (as in modern income analysis) is a function primarily of gross revenue:

> As the capital of an individual can be increased only by what he saves from his annual revenue or his annual gains, so the capital of a society, which is the same with that of all the individuals who compose it, can be increased only in the same manner. . . . It can seldom happen, indeed, that the circumstances of a great nation can be much affected either by the prodigality or misconduct of individuals; the profusion or imprudence of some, being always more than compensated by the frugality and good conduct of others.[20]

Smith's hierarchy of productivity of capital employments provided the theoretical justification for the repudiation of mercantilist policies founded on gains from alienation. Production, not trade, is the real source of wealth. However, Smith's emphasis on the accumulation of durable vendible commodities is consistent with the general mercantilist orientation towards accumulation. The means change but the goal remains. Considered in this light, the utilitarian anti-mercantilist precursors of Adam Smith failed to provide a theory of eco-

[18] *Ibid*., p. 639.
[19] Ibid., p. 329.
[20] *Ibid*., pp. 321 and 324.

nomic progress consistent with the needs of a rising industrial capitalist class. Again, it should be emphasized that general acceptance of a philosophy of utilitarianism was effected through the development of a labour theory of economic value that stressed accumulation.

Smith provided a theory of economic progress. However, Smith's emphasis on the increase of *gross* revenue did not explicitly define the problem of accumulation. The 'gross revenue' concept conceded too much to utilitarianism since it implied a welfare criterion of economic progress.[21] True economic progress consists in augmenting a net revenue that is continually reinvested.[22] The mercantilists understood this better than Smith. Inconsistently, however, Smith did explicitly in one passage of *The Wealth of Nations* identify an increase in gross revenue (value added) with an increase in profits:

> The produce of industry is what it adds to the subject or materials upon which it is employed. In proportion as the value of this produce is great or small, so will likewise be the profits of the employer. But it is only for the sake of profit that any man employs a capital in the support of industry; and he will always, therefore, endeavour to employ it in the support of that industry of which the produce is likely to be of the greatest value. . . .[23]

Here, the value-added criterion is confounded with the net revenue received by the capitalist. What Smith implies is a fixed mark-up on labour (in Marxian terminology 'a constant rate of exploitation') such that the more productively employed capital, that which sets in motion a greater quantity of labour, gains a greater profit. But this passage completely contradicts Smith's theory of a tendency towards an average rate of profit, i.e. equal capitals, regardless of the amount of

[21] In arguing for the accumulation of durable commodities, Smith utilized a welfare standard: 'The houses, the furniture, the clothing of the rich, in a little time, become useful to the inferior and middling ranks of people.' *Ibid.*, p. 330.
[22] Paul Baran (*The Political Economy of Growth*, New York, 1957, pp. 18–19) rightly took issue with Colin Clark's definition of economic progress 'as an improvement in economic welfare'. Baran defined growth as 'an increase over time in *per capita* output of material goods'. But I find Baran's definition also unsatisfactory since, given population growth, the mass of economic surplus can increase without a rise in *per capita* output. This may have occurred at times under mercantilism.
[23] Smith, *op cit.*, p. 423.

value added, will receive equal profits. Further, Smith had previously emphasized:

> The consideration of his own private profit, is the sole motive which determines the owner of any capital to employ it. . . . The different quantities of productive labour which it may put into motion, and the different values which it may add to the annual produce of the land and labour of the society, according as it is employed in one or other of those different ways, never enter into his thoughts.[24]

Actually, Smith indiscriminately employed many different criteria to define productive labour, viz. (1) the increment to gross revenue or value added; (2) net revenue; (3) labour that fixes itself and augments the value of a durable vendible commodity; and (4) labour that fixes itself but merely replaces or maintains the cost of production of the commodity. Now although Smith appeared to believe these criteria identical, they are not. Considered from the point of view of augmenting net revenue, i.e. as a means for further accumulation, it is no matter whether or not labour power fixes itself in a durable vendible commodity. What is of crucial importance is the amount of surplus-value labour power yields, whether employed in services or in the manufacture of durable vendible commodities. Further, as Smith himself admitted in the previously quoted passage, the individual capitalist is interested in *net*, not *gross*, revenue. Smith's view that labour that merely conserves its value in a durable vendible commodity is more 'productive' than the labour of servants which perishes at the moment of production might be defended on the grounds that Smith had in mind the distinction between a stationary and a disinvesting state.

En passant, Smith's confusion of gross and net revenue is analogous to his inconsistently elaborated labour theory of value. Ricardo had taxed Smith for expressing, at one time, the value of a commodity in terms of the amount of labour power it could command (exchange for), and, at another time, stating that commodities exchange according to the amount of labour time required for their production. If following Ricardo, we assume two commodities, *x* and *y*, each requiring eight hours

[24] *Ibid.*, p. 331.

of labour time to produce, the ratio of exchange is one-to-one. Assume further that commodity x is *the wage-good* and subsequently requires (because of diminishing returns in agriculture) 16 hours to produce; as labour time, x now equals $2y$. However, since x is the wage-good and workers must receive a subsistence wage, x cannot command additional labour, although it can command $2y$.

When commodities exchange according to the amount of labour time required for their production, commutative justice prevails. However, equality in exchange requires free competition. Thus, *laissez faire* guarantees commutative justice, which, in turn, is part of Smith's utilitarian rationale. On the other hand, from the point of view of accumulation, the value of commodity capital is the amount of labour power it can command, and this depends upon the net revenue received by the capitalist class. It is this shift in perspective that accounts for Smith's confusion.

Formally considered, Smith's theory of economic progress foundered because of the identification of *net* with *gross* revenue. The result is two theories of profit: On the one hand, through competition, there is a tendency towards an average rate of profit; on the other hand, profit on a particular capital varies directly with the amount of value added. The latter is consistent with Smith's view that profits are a deduction from labour. However, Smith was unable to reconcile his exploitation theory with his theory of a tendency towards an average rate of profit.

But the confusions and contradictions involved do not detract from Smith's eminence. After all, the great Ricardo was unable to reconcile his labour theory of exchange value with an average rate of profit on capital when equal capitals differ in their proportions of fixed and circulating capitals.[25]

[25] Ricardo recognized that if two equal capitals possessed fixed capitals of the same quantity and durability, and their circulating capitals had equal rates of turnover, only then would their produce exchange on the basis of labour time. *On the Principles of Political Economy and Taxation*, third edition, in *The Works and Correspondence of David Ricardo* (edited by Piero Sraffa), Cambridge, 1957, Vol. I, pp. 30 ff. For Marx's solution of the value-price problem, given an average rate of profit and different compositions of capital, see Karl Marx's *Capital* (Kerr edition, Vol. III, pp. 182 ff). See also Paul M. Sweezy, *Theory of Capitalist Development*, New York, 1942, Chapter 7, for an extended discussion of Marx's procedure.

Ricardo accepted Smith's basic distinction between productive and unproductive labour: viz. all labour that exchanges with capital, as distinct from revenue, is productive. However, Ricardo denied Smith's hierarchy of the productivity of capital employments.[26] Ricardo proceeded by distinguishing sharply between gross and net revenue:

> The whole produce of the land and labour of every country is divided into three portions: of these, one portion is devoted to wages, another to profits and the other to rent. It is from the last two portions only, that any deductions can be made for taxes or for savings, the former, if moderate, constituting always the necessary expenses of production. To an individual with a capital of £20,000 per annum, it would be a matter quite indifferent whether the commodity produced sold for £10,000, or for £20,000, provided, in all cases, his profits were not diminished below £2,000. *Is not the real interest of the nation similar?* Provided its net real income, its rent and profits be the same, it is of no importance whether the nation consists of ten or twelve million of inhabitants. Its power of supporting fleets and armies, and all species of unproductive labour, must be in proportion to its net, and not in proportion to its gross income.[27]

Again, in the famous chapter 'On Machinery', which was added in the third edition of the *Principles*, Ricardo recognized that he had been in error in assuming that workers would necessarily benefit from the introduction of machinery:

> My mistake arose from the supposition, that whenever the net income of a society increased, its gross income would also increase; I now, however, see reason to be satisfied that the one fund, from which landlords and capitalists derive their revenue, may increase, while the other, that upon which the labouring class mainly depend, may diminish ... that the same cause which may increase the net revenue of the country, may at the same time render the population redundant, and deteriorate the condition of the labourer.[28]

[26] Ricardo acknowledged that capital employed in agriculture, except on no-rent land, 'puts into motion a greater quantity of labour than an equal capital employed in manufactures and trade'. However, he denied Smith's contention that capital employed in foreign trade puts into motion a smaller quantity of labour than capital employed in domestic trade. *Ibid.*, pp. 350–1.

[27] *Ibid.*, pp. 347–8. (My emphasis.)

[28] *Ibid.*, p. 388. Ricardo quoted with approval from John Barton's *Observations on the Circumstances which Influence the Condition of the Labouring Class of Society* (London, 1817, p. 16) the statement that 'The demand for labour

Ricardo further concluded that the labouring class has a direct interest in unproductive expenditures:

> Independently of the consideration of the discovery and use of machinery . . . the labouring class have no small interest in the manner in which the net income of the country is expended. . . . If a landlord, or a capitalist, expends his revenue in the manner of an ancient baron, in the support of a great number of retainers, or menial servants, he will give employment to much more labour, than if he expended it on fine clothes or costly furniture. . . . If my revenue were £10,000, the same quantity nearly of productive labour would be employed, whether I realised it in fine clothes and costly furniture, &c. &c. or in a quantity of food and clothing of the same value. If, however, I realised my revenue in the first set of commodities, no more labour would be *consequently* employed: I should enjoy my furniture and my clothes, and there would be an end of them; but if I realised my revenue in food and clothing, and my desire was to employ menial servants, all those whom I could so employ with my revenue of £10,000, or with the food and clothing which it would purchase, would be added to the former demand for labourers, and this addition would take place only because I chose this mode of expending my revenue. As the labourers, then, are interested in the demand for labour, they must naturally desire that as much of the revenue as possible should be diverted from expenditure on luxuries, to be expended in the support of menial servants.[29]

[29] *Ibid.*, pp. 392–3.

---

depends on the increasing of circulating, and not fixed capital. Were it true that the proportion between these two sorts of capital is the same at all times . . . it follows that the number of labourers employed is in proportion to the wealth of the State. But such a position has not the semblance of probability. . . . It is easy to conceive that, under certain circumstances, the whole of the annual savings of an industrious people might be added to fixed capital, in which case they would have no effect in increasing the demand for labour.' (pp. 395–6.) It is of interest that Barton denied that an increase in wage rates will augment population. Rather, an increase in real wages leads to the substitution of fixed for circulating capital and hence to a decreased demand for labour. According to Barton, the rapid increase in population in the latter half of the eighteenth century was attributable to a decline in real wages of forty per cent. The decline in real wages, due to the 'increased abundance of precious metals, raises the price of commodities in a greater proportion than the price of labour; it depresses the condition of the labourer, and at the same time increases the gains of his employer, who is thus induced to enlarge his circulating capital . . . to hire as many hands as he has the means to pay . . . this is precisely the state of things most favourable to the increase of people.' Barton, *op. cit.*, pp. 29–30.

The Classical Economists

Ricardo had opened a 'Pandora's box'. The heritage of harmony, predominant in the *Wealth of Nations* in spite of Smith's recognition of conflicts in the field of distribution, was to be succeeded by a heritage of conflict, culminating in the Marxian analysis. Ricardo acknowledged that in the process of accumulation 'Machinery and labour are in constant competition . . .' hence the interests of labour and capital are in conflict. The implications are such as to sanction the destruction of machinery by the workers. Thus, McCulloch, previously persuaded by Ricardo as to the unalloyed beneficial results flowing from the introduction of machinery, wrote to Ricardo, complaining that if Ricardo's new opinion is correct then 'the laws against the Luddites are a disgrace to the Statue book'.[30] Ricardo only emphasized the dilemma when he lamely concluded that:

> The employment of machinery could never be safely discouraged in a State, for if a capital is not allowed to get the greatest net revenue that the use of machinery will afford here, it will be carried abroad. . . . By investing part of a capital in improved machinery, there will be a diminution in the progressive demand for labour; by exporting it to another country, the demand will be wholly annihilated.[31]

Further, given a decline in the demand for labour consequent upon accumulation, it is in the interest of the workers to press for unproductive expenditures. Thus, Ricardo noted that 'a country engaged in war, and which is under the necessity of maintaining large fleets and armies, employs a great many more men than will be employed when the war terminates. . . .'[32] Although it is not in the interests of the workers to press for war, Ricardo recognized that the workers have an interest in unproductive expenditures, i.e. make-work projects that yield a high employment multiplier.

Originally, in his analysis of the process of accumulation, Ricardo had assumed a harmony of interests between workers and capitalists, i.e. gross and net revenue would rise together. The basic conflict of interest was between the landlords and

[30] See Sraffa's introduction to *On the Principles of Political Economy and Taxation, op. cit.*, p. lviii.
[31] *Ibid.*, pp. 396–7.
[32] *Ibid.*, p. 393.

the capitalists. Because in the long-run labour must receive a subsistence wage and because of diminishing returns in agriculture (coupled with tariffs on the importation of grain), it followed that there was a long-run tendency for wages to rise. But since, according to Ricardo, wages and profits vary inversely, and since investment is determined by profits, the landlord class appeared as the sole barrier to accumulation.

However, Ricardo's new opinion on the effect of the introduction of machinery discloses another barrier to accumulation, as well as a conflict between labour and capital. Accumulation leads to a decline in the demand for labour. Accumulation also requires the economizing on unproductive expenditures. But the workers have an interest in unproductive expenditures as a means of increasing the demand for labour. Hence, there is a conflict between employment and accumulation. Ricardo was unable to resolve this dilemma. In his controversy with Malthus over unproductive expenditures, Ricardo, in effect, was forced to disavow his own findings on the conflict between accumulation and employment. Instead, Ricardo had recourse to Say's Law of Markets, i.e. Ricardo regressed to a full employment model, and then proceeded to stress the baneful effects of unproductive expenditures on accumulation.

It will be recalled that Malthus accepted the distinction between productive and unproductive labour.[33] Nevertheless, Malthus argued that since workers were held to a subsistence wage and capitalists tended to accumulate a large share of their income, the unproductive expenditures of the landlords were necessary in order to avoid a general glut of commodities:

> It has appeared then that, in the ordinary state of society, the master producers and capitalists, though they may have the power, have not the will, to consume to the necessary extent. And with regard to their workmen, it must be allowed that, if they possessed the will, they have not the power . . . to those who are inclined to say that unproductive consumers cannot be necessary as a stimulus to the increase of wealth, if the productive classes do but consume a fair proportion of what they produce, I would observe that as a great increase of consumption among

---

[33] *Principles of Political Economy*, reprinted (abridged) in *The Works and Correspondence of David Ricardo*, Vol. II, *Notes on Malthus' Principles of Political Economy, op. cit.*, pp. 15 ff.

the working classes must greatly increase the cost of production, it must lower profits, and diminish or destroy the motive to accumulate. . . . But if the master producers have not the will to consume sufficiently, and the working producers have not the power, then, if the aid of the landlords be not found sufficient, the consumption required must take place among the unproductive labourers of Adam Smith.[34]

Malthus argued for a balance between production and consumption in which the balance struck would be such as to provide an effective demand while, simultaneously, not eliminating accumulation. In short, the landlord class must not accumulate since 'When the demands of the landlords have been added to those of the productive classes, it appears from experience that profits have often prematurely fallen.'[35] The landlords can, however, provide an effective demand without raising costs and hence diminishing profits. This follows from the Ricardian theory of rent because rent does not constitute a part of the supply price of a commodity, i.e. rent is price determined, not price determining.[36] On the other hand, productive workers cannot provide the needed market because of the fundamental dilemma that a rise in wages not only increases demand, but by raising entrepreneurial costs, impedes accumulation.

If we assume that there must be some sort of a balance between production and consumption and, further, if we assume that capitalism has an inherent tendency to accumulate too rapidly, then the Malthusian analysis would be sound. As has already been noted, it follows from the Ricardian theory of rent that the unproductive expenditures of the landlords are not a cost to the capitalists. The landlords, unlike the workers, can help to preserve a balance between consumption and production without blunting the capitalist drive to accumulate.

True, in the very long run, because of diminishing returns

---

[34] *Ibid.*, pp. 429–31.
[35] *Ibid.*, p. 431.
[36] Although in the Ricardian analysis rent is not a social cost, nevertheless a rise in rents means a deduction from surplus value. The landlords gain at the expense of the capitalists, and because of the fall in profits the workers are also injured by a reduced demand for labour. Hence Ricardo's dictum '. . . the interest of the landlord is always opposed to that of the consumer and manufacturer'. *On the Principles of Political Economy and Taxation, op. cit.*, p. 335.

in agriculture, the share of rent in national income will rise. However, the rent phenomenon only reflects the rise in the cost of workers' subsistence—the real barrier to accumulation. In short, provided only that the landlords do not succeed in artificially increasing the cost of subsistence through tariffs, the landlord class is eminently qualified to furnish effective demand without endangering accumulation. It should be stressed, however, that to the extent that rent is price determining (Marx's 'absolute rent') rather than price determined, the preceding analysis must be qualified.

In rejecting the Malthusian thesis of the necessity of unproductive consumers, Ricardo (as has been noted) fell back on Say's Law of Markets. However, Ricardo was not concerned with Malthus' justification of the unproductive expenditures of the landlords. In effect, Ricardo appears to have accepted Malthus' division of labour in which the landlord class was to consume while the capitalist class accumulated. In any event, since rent was not a social cost, Ricardo could not be greatly concerned as to the manner in which the landlord class disposed of its revenue. The fundamental issue for Ricardo was the Malthusian justification for expenditures on unproductive labourers; specifically, Malthus' statement that 'if the aid of the landlords be not sufficient, the consumption required must take place among the unproductive labourers of Adam Smith'.

In the strict Ricardian analysis, the burden of these unproductive expenditures must be carried by the capitalist and landlord classes (labour always tending towards a subsistence wage). Now to the extent that the capitalist class must assume some of the burden of these unproductive expenditures, Ricardo recognized a direct threat to accumulation. The following excerpts from various notes by Ricardo on Malthus' underconsumption doctrine vividly demonstrate Ricardo's reaction:

> A body of unproductive labourers are just as necessary and as useful with a view to future production, as a fire, which should consume in the manufacturers' warehouse the goods which those unproductive labourers would otherwise consume . . . what advantage can it be to me that another man who returns nothing to me shall consume my goods? How does such a consumption enable me to realize my profits? . . . To enable the capitalists to continue their habits of saving says Mr. Malthus

'they must either consume more or produce less'. . . . Commodities consumed by unproductive consumers are given to them, not sold for an equivalent. . . . Will the taking of 100 pieces of cloth from a clothiers manufactury, and clothing soldiers and sailors with it, add to his profits? Will it stimulate him to produce?—yes, in the same way as a fire would. . . . What could be more wise if Mr. Malthus' doctrine be true than to increase the army and double the salaries of all the officers of the government?[37]

We have seen that Malthus' rationale for unproductive expenditures was a deficiency of consumer demand. However, Malthus also provided another argument against excessive accumulation. In discussing the effects of the repayment of the national debt, Malthus wrote:

> It is the greatest mistake to suppose that the landlords and capitalists would either at once, or in a short time, be prepared for so great an additional consumption as such a change would require; and if they adopted the alternative suggested by Mr. Ricardo . . . of saving and lending their increased incomes, the evil would be aggravated tenfold. The new distribution of produce would diminish the demand for the results of productive labour; and if in addition to this, more revenue were to be converted into capital, profits would fall to nothing, and a much greater quantity of capital would emigrate, or be destroyed at home, and a much greater number of persons would be starving for want of employment, than before the extinction of the debt.[38]

Thus, even if there were no problem of effective demand because consumption expenditures would be replaced by invest-

[37] *Ibid.*, pp. 421–5 and p. 450.

[38] *Principles of Political Economy, op. cit.*, p. 435. Previously, Malthus had acknowledged that the upper limit on profits was determined by the rate of profit earned on the least fertile land under cultivation. However, 'limitation is essentially different from regulation. In the descending scale, profits may be lower in any degree. . . . As capital at any time increases faster than labour, the profits of capital will fall, and if a progressive increase of capital were to take place, while the population, by some hidden cause, were prevented from keeping pace with it, notwithstanding the fertility of the soil and plenty of food, then profits would be gradually reduced, until, by successive reductions, the power and will to accumulate had ceased to operate.' *Ibid.*, pp. 257, 259–60. This, of course, is not the Malthus of the *Principles of Population*. Incidentally, Ricardo made the following comment on this passage: 'The labourers would have a monopoly, and the price of their labour would depend solely on the demand.' *Ibid.*, note 166, p. 303.

ment expenditures, nevertheless (since accumulation lowers the rate of profit) additional investment will not long be forthcoming. Such, then, is the Malthusian dilemma of excessive accumulation: Either production outstrips consumption, or, even if production and consumption could be balanced, the fall in the rate of profit consequent upon accumulation chokes off investment.

The doctrine that parsimony must be leavened by consumption goes back to Lauderdale. Lauderdale, who on the basis of a utility theory of value denied any distinction between productive and unproductive expenditures, agreed with Adam Smith that accumulation *per se* lowers the rate of profit on capital. Whereas for Smith the fall in the rate of profit was a natural consequence of opulence and hence desirable, Lauderdale, on the contrary, contended that the fall in the rate of profit consequent upon accumulation meant further investment would cease. For Lauderdale, too rapid accumulation would result in a glut of capital, which would ultimately lead to an actual destruction of capital.

> We already know, that the value of capital may be reduced from 6 to 3 per cent by forced accumulation; and it is impossible to say how low it may be brought, by the continued progress of accumulation, which increases the quantity of capital; whilst, far from increasing (by the effect it has of abstracting revenue from expenditure in consumable commodities, and consequently of abridging consumption), it inevitably diminishes the demand for it . . . it is demonstrable, that before any considerable progress could be made in this system of accumulation, the value of capital must be reduced to a trifle.[39]

Although denying the distinction between productive and unproductive labour, Lauderdale is historically significant in that he first raised the problem of capital saturation. To that extent, Lauderdale's analysis foreshadowed the Marxian theory of the end of accumulation.

Malthus did not follow Smith and Lauderdale in the belief that accumulation *per se* lowered the rate of profit. But Malthus

[39] The Earl of Lauderdale, *An Inquiry into the Nature and Origin of Public Wealth and into the Means and Causes of its Increase*, London, 1804, pp. 265–6; Lauderdale also emphasized the necessity of a balance between production and consumption. Hence, the Malthusian dilemma of accumulation originates in Lauderdale's analysis. *Ibid.*, pp. 208 ff.

did suggest that accumulation might outstrip population growth. Such being the case, wages would rise above their natural level (subsistence) and profits would fall. Given this new assumption about the behaviour of population, Malthus could argue that, even from the point of view of the capitalists, the support of unproductive labourers was not an unmixed evil. By holding back the rate of accumulation, unproductive expenditures checked the fall in the rate of profit. The irony of the controversy lies in Malthus' abandoning his thesis of the *Principles of Population*, whereas Ricardo, accepting the earlier Malthusian analysis, assumed an infinitely elastic supply of labour. Thus, in the Ricardian analysis, as distinct from the Malthusian, profits are not limited but determined by the fertility of the soil.

The under-consumptionist may or may not accept the distinction between productive and unproductive labour. Lauderdale, for example, anticipating Neoclassical analysis, not only denied the distinction but, more positively, formulated a more general view of the co-ordinate contribution of all factors to production, e.g. 'land, labour and capital are, all three, original sources of wealth; that each has its distinct and separate share . . . in the formulation of those objects which are desirable to man and which have been shown to constitute his wealth'. [40]

Again, modern under-consumptionists of the Keynesian persuasion deny any distinction between productive and unproductive expenditures.

On the other hand, the English physiocrat, William Spence, accepted Lauderdale's under-consumptionist thesis:

> Notwithstanding all the declamation which has been made by moralists against the extravagance and profusion of man, it appears, that he is, in fact, much more inclined to **save and to** hoard, than to spend. Hence our land proprietors have never fully performed their duty, they have never expended the whole of their revenue. . . . What the land proprietors have neglected to do, has been accomplished by the national debt. . . . Capital is essential to a nation, but a nation may have too much of it. . . . Expenditure, in short, is the very essence of a system like ours, and what difference can it make to the prosperity of the

[40] *Ibid.*, pp. 111 ff.

country whether it is indebted for this expenditure to the government or the subjects?[41]

John Stuart Mill emphasized the distinction between productive and unproductive labour. Furthermore, unlike his predecessors, Mill recognized that the labour of a teacher must be counted as productive. It was here that Classical political economists had been inconsistent inasmuch as these economists held that labour was a commodity.[42] But if labour is a commodity, then the skills passed on by the teacher to the student fix themselves in a durable vendible commodity:

> I shall ... when speaking of wealth, understand by it only what is called material wealth, and by productive labour only those kinds of exertion which produce utilities embodied in material objects. ... I shall not refuse the appellation productive, to labour which yields no material product as its direct result, provided that an increase of material products is its ultimate consequence. Thus, labour expended in the acquisition of manufacturing skill I class as productive, not in virtue of the skill itself, but of the manufactured products created by the skill, and to the creation of which the labour of learning the trade is essentially conducive. The labour of officers of government, in affording the protection which ... is indispensable to the prosperity of industry, must be classed as productive even of material wealth. ... Such labour may be said to be productive

[41] William Spence, *Britain Independent of Commerce* (London, 1807), p. 71, n. (William Spence should not be confused with his contemporary, Thomas Spence, who advocated land nationalization.) For a summary of physiocracy in Britain see Ronald Meek, 'Physiocracy and Classicism in Britain', *Economic Journal* (March 1951). Spence's thesis was rebutted by James Mill in *Commerce Defended* (London, 1808). Incidentally, Edwin Cannan was in error when he stated that neither James Mill nor Ricardo concerned themselves with the problem of productive versus unproductive expenditures. (*A History of the Theories of Production and Distribution in English Political Economy from 1776 to 1848*, London, 3rd edition, p. 27.) James Mill (*Elements of Political Economy*, London, 1821) distinguished between productive and unproductive consumption: 'What is thus expended for the sake of something to be produced is said to be consumed productively.' (p. 178.) It may be remarked that in my opinion Cannan's discussion of theories of productive and unproductive labour is superficial and misleading.

[42] The omission by the classical economists of teaching as a productive occupation is easily understood. After all, the evolution of production from the handicraft stage, characterized by complex apprenticeship regulations, through the domestic system to the machine fabrication system constituted a secular substitution of unskilled for skilled labour. Hence, Classical economists tended to overlook the cost of education as an element in the supply price of labour.

indirectly or mediately, in opposition to the labour of the ploughman and the cotton spinner, which are productive immediately.[43]

Mill here confounds necessary with productive labour. That is to say, whereas Ricardo progressed beyond Adam Smith and saw that the crucial distinction between productive and unproductive labour rested on the labour-capital relation as distinct from the labour-revenue relation, Mill, by his uncritical acceptance of the durable-vendible-commodity criterion coupled with the 'productive indirectly' qualification, distorts and confuses Smith's basic insight (although inconsistently elaborated by Smith) of the importance of the labour-capital relationship. For Mill, the army, the navy, in short, all of the government bureaucracy, are indirectly productive.

Mill's durable-vendible-commodity criterion is purely utilitarian. The wealth of nations consists of the accumulation of durable commodities that provide 'permanent utilities'. As has been indicated, Mill's criterion constituted a backward step for economic science. His analysis was superficial because it ignored the strategic factor for discriminating between productive and unproductive labour, viz. the labour-capital relation. The utilitarian bias of Mill reflects his basic methodological error, 'trans-temporality'. The analysis abstracts from the specific of capitalist accumulation, namely, net revenue or profit. *En passant*, it may be noted that the classic example of this methodological error (as Marx long ago pointed out) is contained in Mill's dictum that the laws of production are eternal.

Nevertheless, Mill clung to the significance of the distinction between productive and unproductive labour. Further, in discussing the tendency for profits to fall to a minimum, Mill follows Malthus in providing a rationale for unproductive expenditures:

> We have now seen that the lowness of profits is a proof that the spirit of accumulation is so active, and that the increase of capital has proceeded at so rapid a rate as to outstrip the two counter-agencies, improvements in production, and increased supply of cheap necessaries from abroad . . . this view of things

[43] John Stuart Mill, *Principles of Political Economy*, third edition (London, 1852), Vol. I, p. 60.

greatly weakens, in a wealthy and industrious country, the force of the economical argument against the expenditure of public money for really valuable, even though industriously unproductive, purposes. If for any great object of justice or philanthropic policy, such as the industrial regeneration of Ireland, or a comprehensive measure of colonization or of public education, it were proposed to raise a large sum by way of loan, politicians need not demur to the abstraction of so much capital, as tending to dry up the permanent sources of the country's wealth, and to diminish the fund which supplies the subsistence of the labouring population. . . . The abstraction, by raising profits and interest, would give a fresh stimulus to the accumulative principle, which would speedily fill up the vacuum.[44]

In summary, by the formulation of a labour theory of value, classical political economy was able to reconcile the needs of bourgeois accumulation with utilitarianism. However, the synthesis provided by Adam Smith was formally inadequate because Smith confounded the durable-vendible-commodity criterion of productive labour with the capital-labour relation. Further, Smith's value-added criterion for the capital-labour relation ignored the fundamental distinction between gross and net revenue. It remained for Ricardo to emphasize the capital-labour relation as the true criterion of productive labour, i.e. a production-for-profit criterion. But Ricardo's recognition of the strategic value of net rather than gross revenue laid bare the contradictions of political economy. If, with the substitution of machinery, gross revenue fell while net revenue rose, the interests of the workers would be opposed to those of the employers. Further, Ricardo's recognition that workers have an interest in unproductive expenditures raised the issue of a conflict between accumulation and employment.

Malthus' under-consumption doctrine, coupled with the repudiation of his own population doctrine, provided the rationale for unproductive expenditures. Malthus provided two arguments against excessive accumulation, viz., (1) accumulation will outstrip population growth so that the supply-price of labour rises above its cost of production and, consequently, profits must fall; (2) under-consumption, a lack of

---

[44] *Ibid.*, pp. 309–10. For convenience, I have altered slightly the sentence order in the above quotation.

effective demand, is inherent in the capitalist system. Regarding the latter, Malthus argued that the capitalists had too low a propensity to consume. Further, Malthus believed that even the unproductive expenditures of the landlord class might not suffice to provide an adequate demand. Again, Malthus recognized that if wages were increased, this would not solve the problem inasmuch as increased wages lowered profits.

From the point of view of distribution, Malthus' solution of the problem of effective demand by an increase in unproductive expenditures is no solution at all. For an increase in unproductive expenditures, as Ricardo clearly recognized, is tantamount to an increase in the wages bill, i.e. a reduction in profits.

It may be remarked that it would be possible to salvage Malthus' position *vis à vis* Ricardo if we assume that, because accumulation has proceeded faster than population growth, the supply-price of labour has risen above its cost of production and *the workers' propensity to consume has fallen below unity*. In such a case, the solution of the problem of effective demand would be regressive taxation. That is to say, abstractly considered, it would be possible to devise a system of taxation by which the productive workers subsidize the unproductive workers. Malthus, however, did not pursue this line of analysis. Rather, as Ricardo clearly recognized, Malthus would save the profit system by reducing profits and holding back accumulation.

Finally, in John Stuart Mill we find a theoretical justification for Keynesian make-work projects when, as the result of excessive accumulation, we approach the stationary state.

III

SOCIALISTS AND DISSIDENTS

BUT THE TIME APPOINTED for labour is to be narrowly examined, otherwise you may imagine, that since there are only six hours appointed for work, they may fall under a scarcity of necessary provisions. But it is so far from being true, that this time is not sufficient for supplying them with plenty of all things, either necessary or convenient; that it is rather too much; and this you will easily apprehend, if you consider how great a part of all other nations is quite idle. First, women generally do little, who are the half of mankind; and if some few women are diligent, their husbands are idle; then consider the great company of idle priests, and of those that are called religious men; add to these all rich men, chiefly those have estates in land, who are noblemen and gentlemen, together with their families, made up of idle persons, that are kept more for show than use; add to these all those strong and lusty beggars, that go about pretending some disease, in excuse for their begging; and upon the whole account you will find that the number of those by whose labours mankind is supplied, is much less than you perhaps imagined. Then consider how few of those that work are employed in labours that are of real service; for we who measure all things by money, give rise to many trades that are both vain and superfluous, and serve only to support riot and luxury. For if those who work were employed only in such things as the conveniences of life require, there would be such an abundance of them, that the prices of them would so sink, that tradesmen could not be maintained by their gains, if all those who labour about useless things, were set to more profitable employments, and if all they that languish out their lives in sloth and idleness, every one of whom consumes as much as any two of the men that are at work, were forced to labour, you may easily imagine that a small proportion of time would serve for doing all that is either necessary, profitable, or pleasant to mankind, especially while

53

Socialists and Dissidents

pleasure is kept within its due bounds.—Sir Thomas More, *Utopia*, 1516.

(A) THE FRENCH UTOPIANS

MARX AND ENGELS characterized the philosophy and programme of early nineteenth century socialists (Fourier, Saint-Simon and Robert Owen) as 'utopian socialism' in contrast to their own 'scientific socialism'. Utopian socialists believed that socialism could be achieved through reason, propaganda, and example, i.e. the establishment of model communities based on rational principles. Fourier set aside an hour daily for a period of twenty years or so to receive a wealthy sponsor who would provide the necessary capital for his model community. In vain, however! Believing in the progress of reason, the basic goodness of mankind and the enormous benefits to be realized by the application of science to human relations, the utopians appealed to all classes. 'Scientific socialism', on the other hand, while not deprecating the importance of ideas, stresses class conflict as the strategic factor for social change. 'Scientific socialism' relies on the proletariat to usher in the new society.

Charles Fourier (1772–1837) mercilessly criticized the existing commercial society. Moreover, as early as 1805–6 Fourier predicted that competition would lead to monopoly:

> Among the influences tending to restrict man's industrial rights, I will mention the formation of privileged Corporations which, monopolizing a given branch of Industry, arbitrarily close the doors of labour against whomsoever they please. . . . Extremes meet, and the greater the extent to which anarchical competition is carried, the nearer the approach to *universal monopoly*, which is the opposite excess. . . . Monopolies, which operating in conjunction with the great landed interest will reduce the middle and labouring classes to a state of commercial vassalage. . . . The small operators will be reduced to the position of mere agents, working for the mercantile coalition. We shall then see the reappearing of Feudalism in an inverse order, founded on mercantile Leagues, and answering to the Baronial Leagues of the Middle Ages.[1]

The classical economists' distinction between productive

[1] Quoted by Albert Brisbane in his introduction to Fourier's *Theory of Social Organization*, New York, 1876, p. 7.

54

and unproductive labour is implied in Fourier's indictment of the waste inherent in capitalism, specifically in his 'First Waste'. Fourier's catalogue of waste is as follows:

First Waste: Useless or destructive labour. (1) the army (2) the idle rich (3) ne'er-do-wells (4) sharpers (5) prostitutes (6) magistrates (7) police (8) lawyers (9) philosophical cranks (10) bureaucrats (11) spies (12) priests and clergymen.

Second Waste: Misdirected work, since society makes it repellent, and not a vehicle of man's personality, attractive to him.

    (a) Deflection of the passions into greed and morbidity, instead of being utilized as society's motors.

    (b) Scale of production too small to utilize labour properly.

    (c) No co-operation.

    (d) No control of production.

    (e) No adjustment of supply to demand, except by the mechanism of the 'blind' market.

    (f) The family: this economic and educational unit is absurdly small.

Third Waste: Commerce dominated by middlemen. It takes a hundred men to do what society, with warehouses, distributed according to need, could do with one. A hundred men sit at counters, wasting hours waiting for someone to enter, a hundred people write inventories, etc., competitively. These hundred wasted merchants eat without producing.

Fourth Waste: Wage labour in indirect servitude; cost of class antagonisms. Since class interests are opposed, the costs keeping men divided are greater than the gains in making them co-operate.[2]

Fourier concludes that one-third of the people really work at something useful and the other two-thirds, no matter how much they buzz about, do no real work but are parasitic. And even this useful third receive no proper workers' training, due to class corruption and distortion, and so they work poorly.[3]

[2] As summarized by William J. Blake in *Marxian Economic Theory and its Criticism*, New York, 1939, p. 615.

[3] *Ibid.*, p. 615.

Socialists and Dissidents

Saint-Simon's (1760–1825) contribution to Marxian doctrine included a recognition of class conflict, a theory of the withering away of the state, the socialist principle of distribution 'from each according to his capacity, to each what he produces':

It [The French Revolution] was for him a conflict between the Feudal elements, who owned the soil, the bourgeoisie who owned factories and ran commerce, and the poor workers and peasants. Property was at the base of ideas and parties.

Politics, he said later, is merely the science of production and as society becomes more complex, politics as such must fade and disappear into economics. At a time when diplomats and generals were still thought to create history, to have moved its habitation from the salon to the factory and railroad required a prophetic brain. . . . Outside of political economy there are no *socialist* notions in Marx that (apart from their special setting) are not to be found in his works. . . . It was from Saint-Simon that Marx learned that a social structure—a new one, that is— *can be built only on the data of the society that exists*, not of the one that one wishes. . . . Historians like Mignet, Thierry, and Guizot, though bourgeois, took over Saint-Simon's economic and class ideas and remade their science: their perceptions were more significant than those of the technically more advanced Germans like Ranke. Guizot plainly stated that history is class struggle.

It is little wonder that a man like Saint-Simon who opened so many vistas came, after his death, to be regarded by some forty thousand people as the reincarnation of an aspect of Jesus, as the incarnation of social dogma, as Christ was of the Godhead.[4]

Concerning the distinction between productive and unproductive labour, Saint-Simon wrote as follows:

The community has often been compared to a pyramid. I admit that the nation should be composed as a pyramid; I am profoundly convinced that the national pyramid should be crowned by the monarchy, but I assert that from the base of the pyramid to its summit the layers should be composed of more and more precious materials. If we consider the present pyramid, it appears that the base is made of granite, that up to a certain height the layers are composed of valuable materials, but that

[4] *Ibid.*, pp. 617–18.

the upper part, supporting a magnificent diamond, is composed of nothing but plaster and gilt.

The base of the present national pyramid consists of workers in their routine occupations: the first layers above this base are the leaders of industrial enterprises, the scientists who improve the methods of manufacture and widen their application, the artists who give the stamp of good taste to all their products. The upper layers, which I assert to be composed of nothing but plaster, which is easily recognized despite the gilding, are the courtiers, the mass of nobles whether of ancient or recent creation, the idle rich, the governing class from the prime minister to the humblest clerk. The monarchy is the magnificent diamond which crowns the pyramid.[5]

Again,

The Princes, the great household officials, the Bishops, Marshals of France, prefects and idle landowners contribute nothing directly to the progress of the sciences, fine arts and professions. . . . They are harmful because they expend their wealth in a way which is of no direct use to the sciences, fine arts, and professions: they are harmful because they are a charge on the national taxation, to the amount of three or four hundred millions under the heading of appointments, pensions, gifts, compensations, for the upkeep of their activities which are useless to the nation.[6]

(B) THE ENGLISH DISSIDENTS

Early nineteenth-century English critics of *laissez-faire* classical economics—both reformers and socialists alike—grounded their polemics in the distinction between productive and unproductive classes. William Playfair, for example (whom Henryk Grossman termed the first theorist of economic progress[7]) was convinced that societies in their evolution from poverty to wealth are inevitably brought to decay and depopulation through the growth of unproductive expenditures:

Amongst the causes of the decline of wealthy nations, this then is one. The great lose sight of the origin of their wealth, and

[5] *On Social Organization*, in *Henri Comte de Saint-Simon, Selected Writings* edited and translated with an introduction by F. M. H. Markham), Oxford, 1952, pp. 79–80.

[6] *Ibid.*, pp. 73–4.

[7] Henryk Grossman, 'W. Playfair, The Earliest Theorist of Capitalist Development', *The Economic History Review*, Vol. XVIII, Nos. 1 & 2 (1948), pp. 65 ff.

cease to consider, that all wealth originates in labour, and that, therefore, the industrious and productive classes are the sinews of riches and power.[8]

Increased wealth, consequent upon the development of manufactures and trade, results in the substitution of animal for grain diet. Hence, in time, the industrious and productive classes, 'the sinews of riches and power', are decimated since

. . . the same quantity of ground cannot feed the same number of people with animal food. . . . The change that this produces, when once it begins to operate, is a most powerful and effectual cause of decline; and, without the intervention of conquest, or any violent revolution, would of itself be sufficient to impoverish in the first instance, and, in the second, to depopulate a country.[9]

Again:

When nations increase in wealth, the fate of individuals ceases to become an object of attention; and, of all the animals that exist, and are capable of labour, the least value is set upon the human species. . . . One great cause of increase of mendicity is the increase of unproductive labourers, as a state becomes more wealthy, who, dying before their children are able to provide for themselves, increase the number of the indigent. Men living by active industry naturally marry at an early age; menial servants, revenue officers, and all those who administer to the gratification of a wealthy and luxurious people, marry late in life; and besides their not having an industrious example to set before their children, are torn from them sooner by the course of things.[10]

According to Playfair, one could not turn back but one could, at least temporarily, stem the tide of evolution. Hence, Playfair advocated the following: (1) government control over the prices of provisions; (2) progressive taxation on large estates that 'would counteract, to a certain degree, the tendency of landed property to accumulate in any one person's hand'; (3) a law 'compelling all landlords and farmers to have only three-fourths in grass. . . . There would then be always corn in plenty'; (4) repeal of the corn laws but coupled, however, with the *caveat* that free trade 'is a principle not to be adopted

[8] William Playfair, *An Inquiry into the Permanent Causes of the Decline and Fall of Powerful and Wealthy Nations*, London, 1805, p. 133.

[9] *Ibid.*, p. 138.

[10] *Ibid.*, pp. 157–8.

without limitation, but with due regard to times and circumstances; let it never be invoked upon a general question, without examination'.[11]

Finally, Playfair is at his best in his denunciation of the poor laws:

> There is no relief at home in their own houses . . . no, the family must support itself, or go wholesale to the workhouse. This is one of those clumsy rude modes of proceeding that a wealthy people, not overburthen with knowledge, naturally takes to overcome a difficulty, but without care or tenderness for the feelings of those relieved, or that regard for public interest, which ought to go hand in hand. . . . A father and mother, and six children, will cost, at least, fifty pounds in a workhouse; but, perhaps, the aid of twelve or fifteen pounds would keep them from going there, and by that means save the greatest part of the money, while the country, which loses their industry, would be doubly a gainer.[12]

In the same year as Playfair, Charles Hall published his indictment of civilization. Like Playfair, Hall found that the accumulation of wealth meant accumulation of misery. Further, accumulation not only destroys the middle ranks of society but aggravates the condition of the poor because of the growth of unproductive expenditures:

> This increase of wealth or power on the one hand, and poverty and subjection on the other, is brought about not only by those, already in a state of subjection, being placed in a state of still greater subjection; but also because more people are reduced to that state: and this is done by throwing down those people that were a little above the line that divides the rich from the poor, to the other side, or below it; and those also that were poor before are rendered still poorer. And this again is accounted for in this manner: if more men become rich, or those that were rich become richer, the number of unproductive consumers is increased; and many of those that were before consumers, become by these means greater consumers. Hence, consumption is by both means increased, and consequently, poverty.[13]

Hall believed that productive labourers were greatly ex-

[11] *Ibid.*, pp. 148 ff and 281 ff.
[12] *Ibid.*, p. 249.
[13] Charles Hall, M.D., *The Effects of Civilization on the People in European States*, London, 1805, p. 95.

ploited. According to his calculations, productive workers constituted about eight-tenths of the population but 'consumed only one-eighth of the produce of their labour; hence one day in eight or one hour in a day, is all the poor man is allowed to work for himself, his wife and his children'.[14]

Unlike Playfair who did not believe it possible to reverse the tide of progress, Hall was an agrarian. Hall would have strictly limited manufactures and nationalized the land, following which the state would parcel out the land to various families. Only such a plan would ensure to each man the whole product of his labour. Nevertheless, in spite of the utopian quality in Hall's thought, one does find a clearly formulated economic interpretation of the state:

> The wealthy part of these states have in their hands all power; the legislative, the executive, and judiciary, in all their branches, viz. ecclesiastical, magisterial, martial, etc. The poor man, having a vote in certain cases, gives no introduction to any of these; the vote of a poor man being almost always directed by some kind of influence or other of the rich. . . . In the republican government this is more obvious; since, in these times, it is wealth universally that puts power into the hands of those that have it.[15]

It was, however, a conservative, Patrick Colquhoun, who furnished the Ricardian Socialists with the weapon *par excellence* for an attack on classical political economy.[16] Colquhoun was captivated by the economic progress of the British Empire. Interested in political arithmetic, he attempted to quantify the wealth of the British Empire. Colquhoun, however, also was steeped in classical political economy. Hence, in his exposition, Colquhoun provided a table on the number of productive and unproductive labourers in society. It was Colquhoun's table that 'gave the early socialists one-half (the other being the labour theory of value) of their case'.[17] (I reproduce Colquhoun's table because of its interest and inaccessibility.)

[14] *Ibid.*, pp. 117–18.
[15] *Ibid.*, pp. 74–5.
[16] Patrick Colquhoun, *A Treatise on the Wealth, Power, and Resources of the British Empire* . . . London, 1814.
[17] Professor H. L. Beales in a letter to the writer. I am indebted to Beales for first pointing out to me the importance of Colquhoun and for furnishing me with a reproduction of Colquhoun's table.

Socialists and Dissidents

Productive and Unproductive Labour

Productive Labourers, by whose exertions a new Property is created every year.

	Families	Persons	Income £
Agriculture, Mines, etc.	1,302,151	6,129,142	107,246,795
Foreign Commerce, Shipping, Trade, Manufacturers, Fisheries, etc.	1,506,774	7,071,989	183,908,352
Fine Arts	5,000	25,000	1,400,000
	2,813,925	13,226,131	£292,555,147

Unproductive Labourers, whose exertions do not create any new Property.

	Families	Persons	Income £
Royalty, Nobility, Gentry	47,437	316,835	58,923,590
State and Revenue, Army, Navy, Half-pay Pensioners	152,000	1,056,000	34,036,280
Clergy, Law, Physic	56,000	281,500	17,580,000
Schools, Miscellaneous, Universities	45,319	567,937	17,555,355
Paupers	387,100	1,548,400	9,871,000
	687,856	3,870,672	£137,966,225

From: *A Treatise on the Wealth, Power, and Resources, of the British Empire*, in every quarter of the world, including the East Indies: The Rise and Progress of the Funding System explained.

With Observations on the National Resources for the beneficial Employment of a redundant Population, and for rewarding the Military and Naval Officers, Soldiers, and Seamen, for their Services to their Country during the late War. Illustrated by Copious Statistical Tables, constructed on a new plan, and exhibiting a collected view of the different subjects discussed in this work.

by
P. Colquhoun, LL.D.

Referring to the table on productive and unproductive labour, Colquhoun made the following comments indicative of his conservative bias:

> Thus it would appear that more than one-fifth part of the whole community are unproductive labourers, and that these labourers receive from the aggregate labour of the productive classes about one-third part of the new property created annually (however, these unproductive labourers) . . . eminently promote, invigorate, and render more productive the labour of the creating class. . . . It is at the same time equally true, that every state is supported *by the poverty of the community* composing the body politic. Without a large proportion of poverty there could be no riches in any country; since riches are the offspring of labour, while labour can result only from a state of poverty. . . . Poverty is therefore a most necessary and indispensable ingredient in society, without which nations and communities can not exist in a state of civilization. It is the lot of man.[18]

Needless to say, the Ricardian socialists did not derive the same satisfaction from the table on productive and unproductive labour. On the contrary, Colquhoun's table became 'the statistical foundation of the socialist movement'.[19] For example,

> Owen constructed visual aids to illustrate Colquhoun's tables, a set of eight cubes exhibiting a 'General View of Society', the working classes being represented at the base by a large cube whilst the apex was formed by a small cube, representing the Royal family and the aristocracy. . . . John Gray's *A Lecture on Human Happiness* (1825) set out the case that labour received only one-fifth of its produce, the rest being appropriated by the 'unproductive' classes.[20]

[18] *Op. cit.*, pp. 109–10. Immediately following this statement, Colquhoun quotes from his previously published *Treatise on Indigence* (London, 1806, pp. 7–9) the distinction between poverty and indigence: 'The natural source of subsistence is the labour of the individual, while that remains with him he is denominated *poor*; when it fails, in the whole or part, he becomes *indigent*. . . . The great desideratum, therefore is to prop up poverty by judicious arrangements at those critical periods, when it is in danger of descending into indigence.'

[19] H. S. Foxwell in his introduction to Anton Menger's *The Right To The Whole Produce*, London, 1899, p. xliii. See also M. Beer's *A History of British Socialism*, London, 1953 edition, Vol. I, pp. 194, 213, 239, 248, 250.

[20] Asa Briggs 'The Language of "Class" in Early Nineteenth-Century England', in *Essays in Labour History*, edited by Asa Briggs and John Saville, London, 1960, p. 50, n. 1.

Socialists and Dissidents

It is not our intention to retrace well-worn paths and so our discussion of the early socialists is necessarily limited to the importance socialists attached to the distinction between productive and unproductive labour. The importance of this distinction is demonstrated by Asa Briggs in a recent study of the sociology of language. According to Briggs, conservative writers in early nineteenth-century England preferred to speak of the 'ranks' and 'orders' of society, 'but analysts of the distribution of the national income and social critics alike talked increasingly in class terms'.[21] Similarly, the distinction between productive and unproductive labour utilized a different vocabulary:

> There was, however, an influential social cross current which directed attention not to the contrasting fortunes and purposes of 'middle classes' and 'working classes' but to a different division in industrial society, that between 'the industrious classes' and the rest. Those writers who were more impressed by the productive possibilities of large-scale industry than afraid of social 'disintegration' dwelt on this second division. St. Simon's demand for unity of 'the productive classes' against parasitic 'non-producers' had many parallels as well as echoes inside England.[22]

Owen, for example, stated:

> There will be, therefore, at no distant period, a union of the government, aristocracy, and non-producers on the one part and the Industrious Classes, the body of the people generally, on the other part; and the two most formidable powers for good or evil are thus forming.[23]

Once more, the distinction between productive and unproductive labour provided the rationale for the abolition of a system based on man's exploitation of man. Thus, in *The Extraordinary Black Book*, which utilized Colquhoun's tables, it was stated:

> The industrious orders may be compared to the soil, out of which every thing is evolved and produced; the other classes to the

[21] *Ibid.*, p. 49.
[22] *Ibid.*, p. 49.
[23] 'Address to the Sovereign', printed in *The Crisis*, 4 August 1832. Quoted by Briggs, *op. cit.*, p. 50.

trees, tares, weeds and vegetables, drawing their nutriment, supported and maintained on its surface. . . . When mankind attain perfectibility . . . (the useful classes) ought to exist in a perfect state. The other classes have mostly originated in our vices and ignorance . . . having no employment, their name and office will cease in the social state.[24]

Thomas Hodgskin's rejection of the wages fund doctrine led him to a different criterion of productive labour:

It is labour which produces all things as they are wanted, and the only thing which can be stored up or previously prepared is the *skill of the labourer* . . . all the effects usually attributed to accumulation of circulating capital are derived from the *accumulation and storing up of skilled labour.*[25]

As for fixed capital, it is merely the product of previous labour. Further, fixed capital is maintained by living labour. In an eloquent passage that anticipated Marx's 'fetishism of commodities', Hodgskin denied that fixed capital was productive:

One is almost tempted to believe that capital is a sort of cabalistic word, like Church or State, or any other of the general terms which are invented by those who fleece the rest of mankind to conceal the hand that shears them. It is a sort of idol before which men are called upon to prostrate themselves, while the cunning priest from behind the altar, profaning the God whom he pretends to serve, and mocking those sweet sentiments of devotion and gratitude, or those terrible emotions of fear and resentment, one or the other of which seems common to the whole human race, as they are enlightened or wise or ignorant or debased, puts forth his hand to receive and appropriate the offerings which he calls for in the name of religion. . . . The skill and the art of the labourer have been overlooked, and he has been vilified; while the work of his hands has been worshipped.[26]

Similarly, Frederick List, who rejected the abstractions of the classical school in order to ascertain how a particular nation at a particular time could increase in wealth, wrote:

---

[24] *The Extraordinary Black Book* (1831 ed.), pp. 217–18. Quoted by Briggs, *op. cit.*, pp. 50–51.
[25] Thomas Hodgskin, *Labour Defended*, London, 1825, pp. 46 and 49.
[26] *Ibid.*, pp. 60 and 66.

Those who raise pigs, and those who manufacture bagpipes or pills are indeed productive; but the instructors of youth and of manhood, musicians, virtuosos, physicians, judges, and statemen, are productive in a much higher degree. The former produce exchangeable values; the latter, productive power. ... The property of a nation does not depend ... on the quantity of riches and of exchangeable values it possesses, but upon the degree in which productive power is developed.[27]

Finally, Richard Jones, a dissident in that he taxed classical economics for its unhistorical bias, followed Malthus' definition of wealth as consisting of material objects:

A nation, if three-fourths were soldiers or menial servants, would be poor, however fertile the labour of the fourth might be.[28]

Further, Malthus was correct in recognizing that capital was 'wealth saved from revenue with a view to profit'. According to Jones, the importance of distinguishing between capital and revenue is that in many parts of the world workers are supported from revenue and not from capital. Thus, in China workmen 'run about the town from morning to night seeking custom'. Hence these workers are unable to work continuously for any length of time. 'They must ply like a hackney coachman, and when no customer happens to present himself, they must be idle.' What the capitalist does is to ensure continuity of labour since the capitalist can wait for the sale of his product. Also, productivity is increased by the supervision of the capitalist. Again, the capitalist makes possible a greater division of labour.[29]

In summary, pre-Marxian socialists and dissidents emphasized the costs and waste of unproductive expenditures. The indictments were as follows: (1) Growth of unproductive expenditures increases the burden on the productive class. This is morally reprehensible since the unproductive class is parasitic. (2) Growth of unproductive expenditures widens

[27] Frederick List, *The National System of Political Economy* (translated by G. A. Matile), Philadelphia, 1856, pp. 219–20.
[28] *Literary Remains consisting of Lectures and Tracts on Political Economy of the late Rev. Richard Jones* (edited by Rev. William Whewell), London, 1859, p. 346.
[29] *Ibid.*, pp. 383 ff.

the gap between rich and poor. (3) Growth of unproductive expenditures leads to depopulation since (a) substitution of animal for grain diet reduces the supply of food and (b) unproductive labourers have a lower fertility.

But there were exceptions. Thus, Hodgskin objected to defining labour that exchanged with capital, as opposed to revenue, as productive. It is not the accumulation of capital but, rather, the storing up of skilled labour that is productive. On the other hand, according to List, productive labour is that which contributes to the building up of a powerful national economy.

Like the classical economists, pre-Marxist socialists and dissidents emphasized the cost of unproductive expenditures. True, their polemics rested on different premises. Nevertheless, both classical economists and their critics ignored the Malthusian problem of effective demand. The tacit acceptance of Say's Law of Markets retrograded from the physiocratic analysis, specifically Quesnay's Tableau Economique, *where the gaining of a surplus from productive labour is integrated with its realization. Considered thus, all these writers adopted a one-sided and hence limited view of the problems of capital accumulation. Productive expenditures and effective demand are but two sides of the accumulation coin, and no economic analysis can be deemed complete if it fails to appreciate this dualism.*

Marx explicitly recognized the two-fold nature of capitalist accumulation. For Marx, however, this dualism was not merely two facets of an orderly evolutionary process. Rather, in the Marxian analysis, duality is transmuted into the basic contradiction of capitalism. Specifically, the dilemma of capitalist accumulation is the conflict between social production and private appropriation, i.e. production versus consumption. This is the point of departure for the Marxian analysis. However, it is necessary to demonstrate how this basic contradiction manifests itself in the process of accumulation. Here we have but the 'rough notes' out of which Engels was to put together Volumes II and III of Capital.

(C) THE MARXIAN ANALYSIS

Only bourgeois thickheadedness, which regards the capitalist forms of production as its absolute forms—hence as eternal, natural forms of production—can confuse the question as to what is productive labour from the standpoint of capital with the question as to what labour is productive in general, or what is productive labour in general; and consequently fancy itself very wise in giving the answer that all labour which produces anything at all, which has any kind of result, is *eo ipso* productive labour. Only labour *which is directly transformed into capital* is productive. K. Marx, *Theories of Surplus Value* (selections translated from the German by G. A. Bonner and Emile Burns), London, 1951, pp. 177–8.

In the Marxian analysis, the terms 'productive' and 'unproductive' labour are treated as historical categories, i.e. the value or validity of the concepts is determined by the specific problems of the epoch. Thus, when the need for the accumulation of liquid capital was paramount, mercantilist spokesmen were correct in regarding labour that led to the accumulation of treasure as 'productive labour'. In a subsequent period, however, when gains from production dominate, a new category of productive labour arises. The domination of industrial capital over merchant capital—the production of surplus-value rather than its world-wide redistribution—leads to the repudiation of gains by alienation. It is no longer the case that accumulation proceeds on the basis that one man's gain is another's loss. Rather, goods can exchange at value and yet accumulation can occur. Hence, utilizing an historic approach, Marx was able to agree with Ricardo that the capital-labour relation was crucial.

Marx's approach was functional. Does the activity of the worker, *whether in the production of goods or services*, lead to the creation of surplus-value? No matter what the worker produces, his labour is productive if it results in the *creation* of surplus-value. I stress this point since a number of writers have interpreted Marx as an adherent of Smith's durable-vendible-commodity criterion. The following quotations show that this interpretation is erroneous:

. . . one of his [Adam Smith's] greatest scientific merits (as Malthus rightly observed, this critical differentiation between productive and unproductive labour remains the foundation of all bourgeois political economy)—that he defined productive labour as labour *which is exchanged directly with capital*; that is an exchange through which the means of production required for labour, and value in general—money or commodities—are first transformed into capital and labour into wage labour in its scientific meaning. Thereby also what is *unproductive labour* is absolutely defined. It is labour that is not exchanged against capital, but *directly* against revenue, that is, against wages or profit, including of course the various categories of those who share in the profit of the capitalist, as interest and rent. Where all labour in part still pays itself, as for example the agricultural labour of the serfs, and in part is directly exchanged against revenue, as in the case of manufacturing labour in the cities of Asia, there exists no capital and no wage labour in the sense of bourgeois political economy. These definitions are therefore not derived from the material processes of Labour—neither from the nature of its product nor from the work performed as concrete labour—but from the definite social forms, the social relations of production, within which these processes are realized.

An actor, for example, or even a clown, according to this definition is a productive worker, if he works in the employ of a capitalist (an *entrepreneur*) to whom he returns more labour than he receives from him in the form of wages; while a jobbing tailor who comes to the capitalist's house and patches his trousers for him, producing a mere use value for him, is an unproductive worker. The labour of the former is exchanged against capital, that of the latter against revenue. The former produces a surplus value; in the latter, revenue is consumed.[30]

Again,

Again the same labour can be productive, when I buy it as a capitalist, as a producer, in order to make a profit out of it, and unproductive, when I buy it as a consumer, a spender of revenue, in order to consume its use value, no matter whether this use value perishes with the activity of this labour power itself, or realizes, fixes itself in an object.[31]

Once more:

. . . there are certain independent branches of industry, in which the result of the productive process is not a new material

[30] *Theories of Surplus Value, op. cit.*, pp. 153–4.
[31] *Ibid.*, p. 163.

product, not a commodity. Among these, only the industries representing communications, such as transportation proper for commodities and human beings, and the transmission of communications, letters, telegrams, etc., are economically important.[32]

Productive labour produces commodities, i.e. both use values and exchange values; whereas, unproductive labour produces only use values. *But a commodity can be either a good or a service*, e.g. the capitalist purchases labour power not the object labour. Hence, the popular distinction between goods and services is irrelevant for the analysis of productive labour. Thus, Marx speaks of the production of 'immaterial things' as commodities:

> . . . production cannot be separated from the act of its producer, as is the case with all performing artists, actors, teachers, doctors, parsons, etc. Here too the capitalist mode of production is met with only to a small extent, and from the nature of the case can only occur in a few spheres. For example the teachers in educational establishments may be mere wage workers for the *entrepreneur* of the establishment; many such education factories exist in England. Although in relation to the pupils such teachers are not productive workers, they are productive workers in relation to their employer. He exchanges his capital for their labour power, and through this process enriches himself. It is the same with enterprises such as theatres, and other places of entertainment. In such enterprises the relation of the actor to the public is that of an artist, but in relation to his employer he is a productive worker. All these manifestations of capitalist production in this sphere are so insignificant compared with total production that they can be left completely out of account.[33]

In Marx's time these productive services could be legitimately disregarded. However, in the contemporary period, this would not be justified since there has been a secular rise in services as a percentage of consumer budgets. Consider the amount of investment in bowling alleys, stadiums for professional athletic contests (frequently subsidized from the public trough), etc.

Productive labour produces (a) commodities and (b) surplus

[32] *Capital*, Vol. II, p. 61.
[33] *Theories of Surplus Value*, p. 195.

value for the entrepreneur. However, from this it does not follow that all capital-labour relations are productive. On the contrary, expenses of circulation (like rent) are deductions from total surplus value, e.g. the wages and profits earned in radio and television are advertising expenses for industrial capital.

The belief that Marx utilized Smith's durable-vendible-commodity criterion of productive labour apparently stems from Marx's emphasis on material commodity production as the distinguishing characteristic of capitalism. However, when one attends to the architectonic of *Capital*, Marx's distinction between productive and unproductive labour is easily grasped. In Volume I, Marx analyses the process of production, specifically the creation of surplus-value. In Volume II, Marx is concerned with the sale of commodities, i.e. the conditions and expenses involved in realizing on the market the *previously* created surplus-value. Finally, in Volume III, Marx considers capitalist production *in toto*. Such is the general schema of *Capital*. The exposition, of course, is dialectical rather than linear.[34]

In Volume I Marx considers first the formula for a barter economy. Here, the barter relation is given by $W \ldots W$, i.e. commodities (better 'goods' since commodity production implies the existence of money) are exchanged for commodities without the mediation of money.[35] With the introduction of money to facilitate exchange we have the formula $W \ldots M \ldots W$. However, the introduction of money gives the *potentiality* for an interruption of trade. Individual A has sold his commodity to B for money. A now has the alternative of purchasing from C or of hoarding the money he received from

---

[34] 'Marx tells his tale quite in the style of the first-class interesting novelist. He develops the various threads of the story, one at a time, up to some given point, always with an eye to the set purpose of yet further developing the main thread. He will be developing the main thread when, upon reaching a point where it is necessary to understand some contributing thread, or perhaps a number of contributing threads, he will break off the main thread to step aside and develop such other thread or threads; and then, having done this, he will once more pick up the main thread.' W. H. Emmett, *The Marxian Economic Handbook and Glossary*, New York (no date), p. 12.

[35] Following the German text of *Das Kapital*, the symbol 'W' is used to denote a commodity (the German word for which is *Ware*) in order to reserve the symbol 'C' for commodity capital.

B. However, since money here only serves as a means of exchange, rather than as a store of value, it is extremely improbable that A would hoard his money. Nevertheless, the *potentiality* for an interruption of trade now exists. It was for this reason that Marx scorned those economists who accepted Say's Law of Markets.

In the formula, $W \ldots M \ldots W$, money functions merely as a means of exchange. However, it is but a short step from money as a means of exchange to money as capital, e.g. $M \ldots W \ldots M'$, where M' represents an increased quantity of money. The formula $M \ldots W \ldots M'$ subsumes both merchant and industrial capital inasmuch as the formula merely depicts the process of advancing money in order to receive back a greater sum. As such, the formula is too general.

As has been noted, in Volume I Marx is concerned with capitalist production, specifically the creation of surplus-value. Therefore, in order to distinguish gains from alienation (one man's gain is another's loss) from gains through production (creation of surplus-value) Marx utilized the following formula, $C \ldots P \ldots C'$. Here C constitutes industrial capital consisting of means of production, c, and wage payments, v, i.e. $C = c + v$. P represents the production of surplus-value or the value added by the workers. C' is the increased value of industrial capital, i.e. C' consists of $c + v + s$ (surplus value). However, since 'capital is money: Capital is commodities',[36] we can substitute for the commodity formula for the accumulation of capital a money formula, viz. $C \ldots P \ldots C'$ is transformed into $M \ldots C \ldots P \ldots C' \ldots M'$. This, then, is the general formula for the expansion of industrial capital.

The formula $M \ldots W \ldots M'$ is limited to merchant or finance capital. W in the formula for merchant capital is the same as C' in the formula for industrial capital. That is, the industrial capitalist sells C' to the merchant in order to transform his commodity capital into money capital. From the industrial capitalists' point of view, the transaction appears as the $C' \ldots M'$ phase in the process of accumulation, whereas, from the point of view of the merchant capitalists, the transaction appears as the $M \ldots W$ phase in the expansion of merchant capital.

[36] *Capital*, Vol. I, p. 171.

Having differentiated productive and unproductive capital, Marx confines his attention in Volume I to the analysis of the production of surplus-value. However, in Volume II the distinction between productive and unproductive capital (labour) is elaborated:

> Since we have assumed that commodities are bought and sold at their values, these transformations constitute merely a conversion of the same value from one form into another, from the form of commodities into that of money or vice versa. . . . The conversion of a commodity costs time and labour power, not for the purpose of creating values, but in order to accomplish the conversion of value from one form into another . . . the time required for this purpose is an expense of circulation, which does not add any increment to the converted values. . . . If a function, which is unproductive in itself, although a necessary link in reproduction, is transformed by a division of labour from an incidental occupation of many into an exclusive occupation of a few, the character of this function is not changed thereby. One merchant, as an agent promoting the transformation of commodities by assuming the role of a mere buyer and seller, may abbreviate by his operations the time of sale and purchase for many producers. To that extent he may be regarded as a machine which reduces a useless expenditure of energy or helps to set free some time of production.[37]

According to Marx, the expenses of circulation are divided into two general categories: (1) 'Genuine expenses of circulation'; and (2) expenses of circulation that are really part of the production process. Under genuine expenses of circulation, i.e. the expenses of transforming commodity capital into money capital, Marx includes book-keeping, the gold and silver circulating as merchant capital, marketing and correspondence:

> The general law is that *all expenses of circulation, which arise only from changes of form, do not add any value to the commodities.* They are merely expenses required for the realization of value, for its conversion from one form into another. The capital invested in these expenses (including the labour employed by it) belongs to the dead expenses of capitalist production.[38]

Expenses of circulation that are really part of the production

[37] *Ibid.*, Vol. II, pp. 147-9.
[38] *Ibid.*, p. 169.

process merely reflect economies arising from the division of labour: e.g. frequently a merchant capitalist may provide for storage and transportation of commodities as well as performing the purely unproductive labour of buying and selling. Further, the labour the merchant employs in transportation, shipping, packing, sorting, and storage, essential to the production process, yields a surplus-value.

But if capital *qua* merchant capital is unproductive, how does the merchant capitalist accumulate? In the first two volumes of *Capital*, Marx adopted the simplifying assumption that commodities exchange at their values. Given these assumptions, it would be impossible for merchant capital to grow. However in Volume III Marx reconciled the labour theory of value with the facts of an average rate of profit given different compositions of capital, by relating prices of production (cost of production plus an average rate of profit) to values. Marx then showed that the profits of merchant capital constitute a deduction from the mass of surplus-value created by the industrial sector. Hence, other things being equal, the smaller the amount of capital and labour employed in unproductive activities, the greater the profit for industrial capital:

> For this reason, the industrial capitalist endeavours to limit these expenses of circulation to a minimum, just as he does with his expenses of constant capital. Hence industrial capital does not maintain the same relations to its commercial wage labourers that it does to its productive labourers. The greater the number of productive wage labourers employed under otherwise equal circumstances, the more voluminous is production, the greater the surplus-value or profit. . . . The commercial labourer does not produce any surplus-value directly. . . . He adds to the income of the capitalist, not by creating any direct surplus-value, but by helping him to reduce the costs of the realisation of surplus-value.[39]

It will be recalled that the Marxian formula for computing the rate of profit, given an annual turnover of capital, is $\dfrac{s}{c+v}$, where c is embodied labour-time (machinery, buildings, raw materials, etc.), v is the wages bill, and s is the surplus-value

[39] Vol. III, p. 353.

produced. Now according to Marx, the expenses of circulation create no surplus-value, hence they are analogous to a rise in constant capital:

> If the surplus-value s remains constant, while the advanced capital c increases to $c + \Delta c$, then the place of the rate of profit $\dfrac{s}{c}$ is taken by the smaller rate of profit $\dfrac{s}{c + \Delta c}$.[40]

We have seen that in the Marxian analysis, productive labour is not merely labour that exchanges with capital. A further requirement is the production of surplus-value. Hence, the transformation of commodity capital into money capital is recognized as a necessary but unproductive expenditure. Other examples of unproductive activities characterized by a capital-labour relation and obtaining (but diminishing) the average rate of profit, are insurance, finance capital, advertising, etc. Further, the process of production itself may require necessary but unproductive expenses, e.g. a factory may require the services of a night watchman. His salary is a necessary but unproductive expenditure. Now if the company is able to dispense with the service of the night watchman because the government has assumed the protective responsibility, the unproductive nature of the expenditure has not changed. All that has happened is that the burden of the expenditure has been transferred from the corporation to society. Such government expenditures are unproductive. On the other hand, certain nationalized industries are productive, e.g. mining, factory production, etc.

Marx believed that with the progress of capitalism, unproductive expenditures rise both absolutely and relatively:

> ... the extraordinary productiveness of modern industry ... allows of the unproductive employment of a larger and larger part of the working class, and the consequent reproduction, on a constantly extending scale, of the ancient domestic slaves under the name of a servant class, including men-servants, lackeys, etc.[41]

It should be remarked, however, that growth of consumer durable goods such as automobiles, washing machines, vacuum

[40] *Ibid.*, p. 353.
[41] *Ibid.*, Vol. I, p. 487.

cleaners, refrigerators, etc., has a two-fold effect on accumulation. On the one hand, to the extent that such inventions substitute for servants, they economize on surplus-value. The capitalist class has a larger fund available either for investment or for other forms of unproductive expenditures. On the other hand, such inventions aid in recruiting wives into the labour force and thus augment the supply of labour.

For classical economists, productive consumption reflected the distinction between productive and unproductive labour. Similarly, in the Marxian analysis, only the consumption of wage earners who yield a surplus-value is productive consumption. As Sraffa has pointed out:

> It is of course in Quesnay's *Tableau Economique* that is found the original picture of the system of production and consumption as a circular process, and it stands in striking contrast to the view presented by modern theory, of a one-way avenue that leads from 'Factors of production' to 'Consumption goods.'[42]

It will be recalled that in the Ricardo-Malthus debate on the effects of accumulation, Malthus stressed the necessity of a growth in unproductive expenditure to achieve a balance between production and consumption. Now Marx, of course, did not accept the Malthusian solution. In fact, Marx noted sarcastically that

> In order to charm out of his bosom the awful conflict between the desire for enjoyment and the chase after riches, Malthus, about the year 1820, advocated a division of labour, which assigns to the capitalist actually engaged in production, the business of accumulating, and to the other sharers in surplus-value, to the landlords, the place-men, the beneficed clergy, etc., the business of spending. It is of the highest importance, he says, 'to keep separate the passion for expenditure and the passion for accumulation.'[43]

Accumulation and Effective Demand

In Volume II of *Capital*, after having examined the unproductive expenditures involved in the transformation of commodity capital into money capital, Marx considers in detail

[42] Piero Sraffa, *Production of Commodities By Means of Commodities*, London, 1960, p. 93.
[43] *Capital*, Vol. I, pp. 652–3.

Socialists and Dissidents

the remaining conditions requiring fulfilment before commodity capital can be transformed into money capital. The procedure is as follows: first, Marx considers the equilibrium conditions for simple reproduction, i.e. no net investment; secondly, Marx analyses the equilibrium conditions for expanded reproduction (balanced growth).[44]

The equilibrium condition for simple reproduction—supply equals demand—is derived from the following equations:

$$
\begin{array}{lll}
& \text{Production of} & \text{Realization of} \\
& \text{Surplus Value} & \text{Surplus Value} \\
& \text{(Supply)} & \text{(Demand)} \\
\text{I (Producer Goods)} & C_1 + V_1 + S_1 & = & C_1 + C_2 \\
\text{II (Consumer Goods)} & C_2 + V_2 + S_2 & = & V_1 + V_2 + S_1 + S_2
\end{array}
$$

For simplicity, Marx assumed that all of the constant and variable capital were utilized and replaced during the accounting period. Further, under simple reproduction both capitalists and workers must consume all of their income. The equilibrium condition for simple reproduction, $V_1 + S_1 = C_2$, is found by cancelling identical terms in the above equations.

The equilibrium condition for expanded reproduction (balanced growth), given the previous assumption that all constant and variable capitals consumed in the previous period are replaced, can be expressed as follows:

$$
\begin{array}{lll}
\text{Production of Surplus Value} & \text{Realization of Surplus Value} \\
\text{(Supply)} & \text{(Demand)} \\
\text{I (Producer Goods)} & \\
dC_1 + dV_1 + dK_1 & = & dC_1 + dC_2 \\
\text{II (Consumer Goods)} & \\
dC_2 + dV_2 + dK_2 & = & dV_1 + dV_2 + dK_1 + dK_2
\end{array}
$$

Where 'd' stands for increments to constant capital (dC), to variable capital (dV), and to capitalists' consumption (dK) from surplus-value. (As in simple reproduction, it is assumed that workers consume all of their income.) Again, the equilibrium condition for balanced growth, $dC_2 = dV_1 + dK_1$, is found by cancelling identical terms in the above equations. Here Marx utilized Say's Law of Markets in order to emphasize that even if all saving is reinvested, there remains an additional constraint for balanced growth, e.g. some entrepreneurs are in

[44] *Ibid.*, Vol. II, Chapters XX and XXI.

76

for a disappointment if (say) increased investment in the consumer goods sector (dC_2) is not matched by increased consumption expenditures of workers and capitalists in sector I ($dV_1 + dK_1$). Again, if we abstract from changes in wage payments in the producer goods sector, it is obvious that increased investment (saving) in the consumer goods sector requires increased consumption expenditures by the capitalists in the producer goods sector. Modern advocates of a high consumption economy ignore this relationship. Stated otherwise, *the 'optimum propensity to consume' is given by the equilibrium condition $dC_2 = dV_1 + dK_1$.*[45]

As has been indicated, Marx did not accept Malthus' growth of unproductive expenditures as a solution to the problem of effective demand. However, after pointing out that 'The premise of simple reproduction . . . is irreconcilable with capitalist production,' Marx does mention *en passant* that '. . . considering the natural growth of total population per year, simple reproduction [with full employment?] could take place only in so far as a correspondingly larger number of unproductive servants could partake of . . . the aggregate surplus production. But accumulation of capital, actual capitalist production, would be impossible under such circumstances.'[46]

True, there is a conflict between production and consumption in the Marxian analysis. The relations of production determine distribution, which in turn defines the limits of consumption. But since for Marx the relations of production are funda-

---

[45] Oscar Lange follows the Keynesian procedure of lumping together investment expenditures of both sectors. Not only does Lange ignore the disaggregation problem but, in the stagnation tradition Lange assumes that investment is a function of consumer expenditures and the rate of interest. 'The Rate of Interest and the Optimum Propensity to Consume', *Economica*, Volume V (new series), Number 17, reprinted in *Readings in Business Cycle Theory* (Selected by a Committee of the American Economic Association), Philadelphia, 1944, pp. 169 ff.

[46] *Capital*, Vol. II, p. 608. Simple reproduction is incompatible with capitalism since 'If the total capital employed in the machine-building industry were even only large enough to replace the annual wear and tear of machinery, it would produce more machinery than it required each year, since in part the wear and tear is conventional and in reality only has to be replaced *in natura* after a certain period of years. . . . In order that this capital should continue in motion and merely reproduce itself continuously each year, a continuous new extension of the industry which uses these machines is required. . . . Here therefore, even *if in this sphere of production the capital invested in it is only reproduced*, continuous accumulation in other spheres of production is necessary.' *Theories of Surplus Value*, p. 355.

Socialists and Dissidents

mental, attempts to raise the community's average propensity to consume are dismissed as Utopian:

> ... Malthus brings in as a 'remedy', a class which buys without selling and consumes without producing, receives in the first instance a considerable portion of the value of the annual product without *paying* for it, and enriches the producers by virtue of the fact that the latter, having first had to cede to it gratuitously the money required for the purchase of their commodities, subsequently appropriate this money once more by selling their commodities above their value to this class, thus receiving back from it more value in the form of money than they supply to it in the form of commodities. And this transaction goes on repeating itself every year ... we have an immense section of society which consists of parasites and self-indulgent drones, in part masters and in part servants, who appropriate gratuitously a considerable quantity of wealth— partly under the name of rent and partly under political titles— from the capitalist class, paying for the commodities produced by the latter above their value with the money they have taken from the capitalists themselves.[47]

The Heresy of Underconsumption

The underconsumption thesis continued to haunt Marxists. Thus, we find Rosa Luxembourg accepting Marx's thesis that the growth of non-productive consumers within a country is no solution inasmuch as these non-productive consumers share in surplus-value and hence depress profits. Nevertheless, utilizing Marx's two-departmental scheme, Rosa Luxembourg came to the conclusion that capitalism required a foreign market to compensate for under-consumption at home. According to Luxembourg, the real meaning of imperialism is the search for foreign markets. In fact, Luxembourg went so far as to assert the impossibility of accumulation within a country:

> The decisive fact is that the surplus value cannot be realized by sale either to workers or to capitalists, but only if it sold to such social organizations or strata whose own mode of production is not capitalistic. ... The enormous expansion of the English cotton industry was thus founded on consumption by non-

[47] *Theories of Surplus Value*, Vol. III, quoted in *Marx and Engels on Malthus* (edited by Ronald L. Meek), London, 1953, pp. 156–8.

78

capitalist strata and countries . . . Conversely, capitalist production supplies means of production in excess of its own demand and finds buyers in non-capitalist countries. English industry, for instance, in the first half of the nineteenth century supplied materials for the construction of railroads in the American and Australian states.[48]

Luxembourg's curious theory of underconsumption was derived from the following propositions: (1) The demand for the output of Department I (constant capital) could only equal the expenditures on constant capital at the beginning of the production period, i.e. *ex post* demand must equal *ex ante* outlays; and (2) the demand for the output of Department II (consumer goods) also could consist only of the expenditures on variable capital advanced at the beginning of the production period plus the consumption of the capitalist class:

> They [workers and capitalists] can always only realize the variable capital, that part of the constant capital which will be used up, and the part of the surplus value which will be consumed, but in this way they merely ensure that production can be renewed on its previous scale. The workers and capitalists themselves cannot possibly realize that part of the surplus value which is to be capitalized.[49]

In Russia, the Narodnik economists had anticipated Luxembourg's criticism of Marx's two-department scheme of expanded reproduction. According to these economists, capitalism could not develop in Russia since (1) the development of capitalism in agriculture destroys the peasantry and hence the home market and (2) 'the foreign market is closed to a young country that has entered the path of capitalist development too late'.[50]

Lenin's criticism of the Narodnik economists also utilized Marx's two-department scheme. True, the development of capitalism in agriculture destroys the peasantry but, following Marx, Lenin went on to show how the process of accumulation creates the home market. The details of Lenin's exposition need not detain us. It suffices to note that Lenin applied Marx's

[48] Rosa Luxembourg, *The Accumulation of Capital* (translated by Agnes Schwarzschild), London and New Haven, 1951, pp. 351–3.

[49] *Ibid.*, p. 350.

[50] V. I. Lenin, *The Development of Capitalism in Russia*, Moscow: Foreign Languages Publishing House, 1956, p. 19.

theory of expanded reproduction in an exhaustive study of the specifics of capitalist development in tsarist Russia. Basic to Lenin's polemic was the recognition that accumulation could achieve temporary independence of consumption:

> According . . . to the general law of capitalist production, constant capital grows faster than variable capital. Hence, constant capital in articles of consumption has to increase faster than variable capital and surplus-value in articles of consumption, while constant capital in means of production has to increase fastest of all, outstripping both the increase of variable capital (plus surplus-value) in means of production and the increase of constant capital in articles of consumption. The department of social production which produces means of production has, consequently, to grow faster than the one which produces articles of consumption. Thus the growth of the home market for capitalism is to a certain extent 'independent' of the growth of personal consumption, taking place in greater measure on account of productive consumption. But it would be a mistake to understand this 'independence' as meaning that productive consumption is entirely divorced from personal consumption: the former can and must increase faster than the latter (and there its 'independence' ends), but it goes without saying that, in the last analysis, productive consumption is always bound up with personal consumption. . . . Marx's analysis of realization showed that 'in the last analysis, the circulation between constant capital and constant capital is limited by personal consumption'; but this same analysis showed the true character of this 'limitedness', it showed that, compared with means of production, articles of consumption play a minor role in the formation of the home market . . . there is nothing more absurd than to conclude from the contradictions of capitalism that the latter is impossible, non-progressive, and so on—to do that is to take refuge in the transcendental heights of romantic dreams away from unpleasant, but undoubted realities.[51]

The thesis that capitalist development is characterized by a rise in the capital-labour ratio means that Department I must grow more rapidly than II. Further, Lenin is correct in stating that investment can achieve temporary 'independence' from consumption. However, Lenin was in error when he concluded that 'constant capital in means of production has to increase

[51] *Ibid.*, pp. 31–6.

fastest of all, outstripping both the increase in variable capital (plus surplus-value) in means of production and the increase of constant capital in articles of consumption'.

The net output of Department I consists of constant capital destined for reinvestment within Department I and constant capital destined to serve as means of production in Department II. The constraints in the Marxian model are as follows: (1) the overall capital-labour ratio is rising, hence Department I grows more rapidly than II; (2) the equilibrium condition for balanced growth requires that $dC_2 = dV_1 + dK_1$. From these constraints it cannot be deduced that constant capital in I grows more rapidly than constant capital in II. Formally considered, a rise in the overall capital-labour ratio is consistent with a falling capital-labour ratio in I. E.g. assume for simplicity that the propensity to save (invest) of entrepreneurs is unity.[52] The equilibrium condition for growth now becomes $dC_2 = dV_1$. Thus if the overall rise in the capital-labour ratio occurs as a result of a rise in the capital-labour ratio in II, we obtain the following conclusions: (1) constant capital in Department I grows more rapidly than variable capital in II, (2) variable capital in sector I must grow at the same rate as constant capital in II; and since C_2 grows more rapidly than V_2, it follows that V_1 must grow more rapidly than V_2. Similarly, if we introduce capitalist consumption, constant capital in I must grow more rapidly than the sum of variable capital and entrepreneurial consumption in II; and $V_1 + K_1$ must increase more rapidly than $V_2 + K_2$.[53] If the rise in the overall capital-labour ratio occurs because C_2

---

[52] cf. Joan Robinson, *The Accumulation of Capital*, London, 1958, pp. 74 ff.

[53] 1. $dC_1 + dV_1 > dC_2 + dV_2$ Department I grows more rapidly than II.
2. $dV_1 = dC_2$ Equilibrium growth condition.
3. $\therefore dC_1 > dV_2$ Cancelling dV_1 and dC_2 in 1.
Now assume the overall rise in the capital-labour ratio occurs because of a more rapid rate of growth of constant capital in II so
4. $dC_2 > dC_1$
5. $\therefore dV_1 > dV_2$ from 1 and 4.
6. $\therefore dV_1 > dC_1$ from 2 and 4.
i.e. the capital-labour ratio in department I must fall. Similarly, if we include capitalist consumption
1. $dC_1 + dV_1 + dK_1 > dC_2 + dV_2 + dK_2$ Department I grows more rapidly than II.
2. $dV_1 + dK_1 = dC_2$ Equilibrium growth condition.
3. $dC_1 > dV_2 + dK_2$ Cancelling $dV_1 + dK_1$ and dC_2 in 1.

increases more rapidly than C_1, then V_1 (or $V_1 + K_1$) must increase more rapidly than V_2 (or $V_2 + K_2$). This law is an important tool for the economic analysis of cyclical phenomena.

Preliminary Remarks on Departmental Analysis and the Process of Capitalist Industrialization

According to W. C. Hoffmann, the growth morphology of industrial market economies is as follows:

> Whatever the relative amounts of the factors of production, whatever the location factors, whatever the state of technology, the structure of the manufacturing sector of the economy has always followed a uniform pattern. The food, textile, leather and furnitures industries—which we define as 'consumer-goods industries'—always develop first during the process of industrialization. But the metal-working, vehicle building, engineering and chemical industries—the 'capital-goods industries'—soon develop faster than the first group. This can be seen throughout the process of industrialization. Consequently the ratio of the net output (value added) of the consumer-goods industries continually declines as compared with the net output of the capital-goods industries. . . . For the purposes of our analysis we have divided this gradual process into the following four stages. . . . In Stage I the consumer-goods industries are of overwhelming importance, their net output being on the average five times as large as that of the capital-goods industries. In Stage II the initial lead of the consumer-goods industries has diminished to a point where their net output is only two and one-half times as large as that of the capital-goods industries. In Stage III the net output of the two groups of industries are approximately equal and in Stage IV the consumer-goods industries have been left far behind by the rapidly growing capital-goods industries. The main purpose of this book is to show that these stages of economic development can be identified for all free economies. Only brief references are made to the industrial expansion of Soviet Russia.[54]

[54] W. G. Hoffmann, *The Growth of Industrial Economies* (translated by W. O. Henderson and W. H. Chaloner), New York, 1958, pp. 2–3.

Now assume the overall rise in capital-labour ratio occurs because of a more rapid rate of growth of constant capital in II so

4. $dC_2 > dC_1$
5. $\therefore dV_1 + dK_1 > dV_2 + dK_2$ from 1 and 4.
6. $\therefore dV_1 + dK_1 > dC_1$ from 2 and 4.

Socialists and Dissidents

Hoffmann's first proposition that industrialization begins in the consumer sector is undoubtedly correct. However, Hoffmann's second proposition that industrial market economies ultimately reach a stage where net output of capital-goods exceeds consumer-goods requires further examination.

First, however, it should be pointed out that Marx's numerical examples of expanded reproduction also assume that the output of the investment sector can exceed the output of the consumer sector. Subsequent expositors of Marxian thought also made this assumption. Since the capital-labour ratio rises secularly (sector I grows more rapidly than II), extrapolation of the trend leads to the apparent result that net output of I can exceed II. But it can be shown that this is impossible without revolutionary changes in income distribution incompatible with the capitalist system. Consider the following numerical example:

Net Value of I's Output $1200.00		Net Value of II's Output $1000.00	
Profits	660.00	Profits	540.00
Wages	540.00	Wages	460.00
Demand for I's Output $1200.00		Demand for II's Output $1000.00	
I's Profits	660.00	I's Wages	540.00
II's Profits	540.00	II's Wages	460.00

In this hypothetical case, profits would have to exceed 50 per cent of national income. And the profit-takers are not even permitted to eat!

United States national income statistics indicate that labour's share of national income has ranged from 60 to 70 per cent during the past several decades. In periods of prosperity labour's share declines, as would be expected, since investment rises as a per cent of national output. Conversely, during periods of depression when investment and profits fall, labour's share rises. Of course, this does not mean that labour welcomes a depression. Obviously, 60 per cent of 100 billion is preferable to 70 per cent of 50 billion.

These statistics on national income distribution suggest a

83

ceiling or limit on the ratio of the net output of investment to consumer goods. Absolute precision is, of course, impossible. However, assume that during prosperity profits are 40 per cent of national income and that 50 per cent of the profits are consumed and the remainder invested. This gives the following arithmetical result:

Net Value of I's		Net Value of II's	
Output	$200.00	Output	$800.00
Profits	80.00	Profits	320.00
Wages	120.00	Wages	480.00
Demand for I's		Demand for II's	
Output	$200.00	Output	$800.00
½ Profits of I are	40.00	½ Profits of I are	40.00
½ Profits of II are	160.00	½ Profits of II are	160.00
		Wages from I are	120.00
		Wages from II are	480.00

In this example, the ratio of investment to consumer goods is 1 to 4, or stated otherwise, net investment is 20 per cent of national output.

As was indicated, I do not claim precision for the above numerical example. But the example does indicate that a continued rise in the ratio of investment to consumer goods would require a fantastic increase in profits at the expense of wages.[55] Here, then, is a suggested limit or ceiling on the rise in the ratio of investment to consumer output—a ceiling incompatible with Hoffmann's data or the usual numerical examples found in Marxian literature.

Although I cannot, as yet, develop the argument in detail, it is possible on the basis of our numerical examples to anticipate the basic dilemma of capitalist accumulation: *Either insufficient profits to continue the process of investment, or, given a boom in the consumer sector, the fall in labour's share in national income during prosperity precipitates a crisis of over-*

---

[55] In Henryk Grossman's model, which assumes sector I exceeds II, accumulation is brought to a halt through a profit shortage, *Das Akkumulations-und Zusammenbruchsgesetz des Kapitalistischen Systems*, Leipzig, 1929, Chapter 2, pp. 78 ff.

production in the consumer sector. But more of this later.

Sectoral Analysis of the First Stage of Industrialization
In the initial stage of industrialization, investment is directed mainly to the consumer goods sector. The contribution of the producer goods sector to total output varies from 15 to 25 per cent.[56] Marx depicted the evolution of capitalism (sectoral changes) as follows:

> Modern Industry had therefore itself to take in hand the machine, its characteristic instrument of production, and to construct machines by machines. It was not until it did this, that it built up for itself a fitting technical foundation, and stood on its own feet. Machinery, simultaneously with the increasing use of it, in the first decades of this century, appropriated by degrees, the fabrication of machines proper. But it was only in the decade preceding 1866, that the construction of railways and ocean steamers on a stupendous scale called into existence the cyclopean machines now employed in the construction of prime movers. . . . So long as . . . the factory system extends itself at the expense of the old handicrafts or of manufacture, the result is as sure as is the result of an encounter between any army furnished with breach-loaders, and one armed with bows and arrows. This first period, during which machinery conquers its field of action, is of decisive importance owing to the extraordinary profits that it helps to produce. . . . So soon, however, as the factory system has gained a certain breadth of footing and a definite degree of maturity, and, especially, so soon as its technical basis, machinery, is itself produced by machinery; so soon as coal mining and iron mining, the metal industries, and the means of transport have been revolutionized; so soon, in short, as the general conditions requisite for production by the modern industrial system have been established, this mode of production acquires an elasticity, a capacity for sudden extension by leaps and bounds that finds no hindrance except in the supply of raw material and in the disposal of the produce.[57]

For the early stage of industrialization, the higher capital-labour ratio in the consumer goods sector is also confirmed by a demand-for-labour analysis. Investment in the consumer goods sector, especially the textile industry, meant not only the

[56] Hoffmann, *op. cit.*, p. 2.
[57] *Capital*, Vol. I, pp. 420 and 492.

substitution of capital for labour. Rather, an essential part of the process of mechanization (and one that, I believe, has received insufficient recognition in theoretical works on capitalist dyanamics) was the substitution of the less costly labour power of women and children for that of adult male handicraftsmen.[58] In short, greater investment in the consumer goods sector coupled with the depreciation of the value (cost) of labour-power raises the organic composition of capital in sector II. Conversely, prior to the mechanization of the producer goods sector, the value of labour-power of artisans employed in the fabrication of means of production is of a higher quality (cost) *vis à vis* employees in the consumer goods sector. Now we have it on Marx's authority that skilled labour can be analytically resolved into multiples of unskilled labour.[59] Hence, not only greater investment in the consumer goods sector but qualitative changes in the demand for labour raise the capital-labour ratio in the consumer goods sector.[60]

Consider now the implications of a more rapid rate of growth of constant capital in the consumer goods than in the producer goods sector. The equilibrium condition for balanced growth is given by the equation $dC_2 = dV_1 + dK_1$. Hence, given that sector I grows more rapidly than II, if C_2 grows more rapidly than C_1, effective demand for the output of the consumer goods sector requires either a fall in the capital-labour ratio in sector I and/or a rise in consumption expenditures by the entrepreneurs of sector I.

We can dismiss the possibility of a significant rise in con-

[58] See my *Population Theories and the Economic Interpretation*, London, 1957, Chapter VIII, 'The Demand for Labour'. Incidentally, it is axiomatic in contemporary economic texts that *cet. par.* a rise in wages leads to the substitution of capital for labour. But an overall rise in wages might increase the cost of machinery more than the cost of wage goods, in which case the relative price of machinery rises. (But see below, pp. 96–7, for a more extended discussion of the substitution effect.) However, to the extent that technological progress represents the substitution of less costly labour-power, it is obvious that even if average real wages were falling it could still pay to substitute capital for labour. That is to say, the substitution of capital for labour in the initial period of industrialization entailed the substitution of unskilled for skilled labour.

[59] *Capital*, Vol. I, pp. 51–2.

[60] 'Various factors restrict the expansion of the capital-goods industries in the early Industrial Revolution. The new capital goods industries required not only large amounts of capital but also a high proportion of skilled workers while the new consumer goods industries generally use relatively unskilled or easily-trained workers and less capital.' W. G. Hoffmann, *op. cit.*, p. 32.

sumption expenditures by entrepreneurs in sector I inasmuch as the ethos of the early period of industrialization was thrift-oriented.[61] (This ethos, of course, reflected the needs of a class of capitalist employers 'as yet in its infancy'.) Regarding consumption expenditures of entrepreneurs, it seems reasonable to conclude that consumption expenditures rose absolutely but declined relatively, i.e. the average propensity to save of entrepreneurs was rising. What then of the possibility of a fall in the capital-labour ratio in sector I? We have seen that qualitative changes in demand for labour, the fabrication of producer goods by skilled labour, may have reduced the capital-labour ratio in sector I. Similarly, quantitative changes in demand for labour in sector I determine the capital-labour ratio. As Marx himself pointed out in his discussion of the first period of industrialization,

> ... the immediate effect of machinery is to increase the supply of raw material in the same way, for example, as the cotton gin augmented the production of cotton. On the other hand, the cheapness of the articles produced by machinery, and the improved means of transport and communication furnish the weapons for conquering foreign markets. By ruining handicraft production in other countries, machinery forcibly converts them into fields for the supply of its raw material. In this way East India was compelled to produce cotton, wool, hemp, jute, and indigo for Great Britain. By constantly making a part of the hands 'supernumerary', modern industry in all countries where it has taken root, gives a spur to emigration and to the colonization of foreign lands, which are thereby converted into settlements for growing the raw material of the mother country; just as Australia, for example, was converted into a colony for growing wool. A new and international division of labour, a division suited to the requirements of the chief centres of modern industry, springs up, and converts one part of the globe into a chiefly agricultural field of production, for supplying the other part which remains a chiefly industrial field.[62]

In the first stage of industrialization, then, the tendency was for a rise in the capital-labour ratio in sector II: First, because

---

[61] Further, the constraint that the producer goods sector must grow more rapidly than the consumer goods sector sets a limit to entrepreneurial expenditures on consumption.

[62] *Capital*, Vol. I, p. 493.

mechanization proceeded initially in the consumer goods sector and was accompanied by the substitution of unskilled for skilled labour; and second, prior to the mechanization of the production of means of production, sector I utilized labour of a higher quality (cost). The latter effect, however, was counteracted to the extent that the international division of labour converted 'one part of the globe into a chiefly agricultural field of production, for supplying the other part which remains a chiefly industrial field'.

The overall tendency was for constant capital to increase more rapidly in II than in I. The equilibrium condition for balanced growth requires that $V_1 + K_1$ grow *pari passu* with C_2. But a market economy—'atomistic diffusion of productive decisions among numerous autonomous entrepreneurs'[63]— provides no guarantee that such will be the case. On balance, it seems reasonable to conclude that sectoral equilibrium was effected mainly through crises of overproduction originating in Department II. Rostow, for example, reaches a similar conclusion regarding the characteristic feature of early business cycles in England. However, it should be obvious that Rostow's emphasis on foreign trade is not central to our argument:

> . . . minor cycles tend, virtually, to disappear . . . after 1860, excepting, of course, the special case of 1907. . . . The euthanasia of minor cycles presents, in fact, no great analytic mystery. The minor cycles are distinguished here by the fact that they involved increases in production and employment arising preponderantly, but not exclusively, from increases in exports. In the first half of the nineteenth century textiles and other consumers' goods constituted the dominant element in British exports. . . . Until the sixties . . . the short cycle can not only be detected but . . . it had sufficient power to produce distinguishable general movements in total production and employment.
>
> As industrialization progressed, however, and the metallurgical and engineering industries began to play an increased proportional role in the economy, the long-term investment cycle became increasingly dominant. This was the trend not only for Britain, but for certain key British markets on the continent and in the United States; and thus the longer rhythm

[63] Maurice Dobb, *Political Economy and Capitalism*, New York, 1937, pp. 79–80.

—the nine-year average—infected not only British domestic activities, but foreign trade as well.[64]

The preceding discussion indicates that a fruitful line of enquiry into the evolution of capitalism would proceed to deliniate periods or stages of capitalism by comparing rates of growth of constant capital between the two departments. Such a criterion suggests the hypothesis that in the initial period of capitalist industrialization, characterized by a more rapid growth of constant capital in the consumer goods sector, the tendency was toward short and regular cycles of over-production of consumer goods. This tendency, of course, was counteracted by the business cycle. In short, in the initial period of industrialization, there was a chronic tendency for dC_2 to exceed $dV_1 + dK_1$.

Incidentally, when Marxists change their perspective and contrast capitalist and socialist processes of industrialization, they recognize that the capital-labour ratio rises more in the consumer goods sector in the first phase. It is in this context that a decisive advantage is claimed for socialist industrialization since development of the producer goods sector does not have to await accumulation in the consumer goods sector.

Sectoral Analysis of the Second Stage of Industrialization

In the second stage of industrialization, the ratio of C_1 to C_2 rises. Heavy investment in the producer goods sector, a rise in the capital-labour ratio, introduces temporary stability into the system. In terms of the equilibrium growth condition, the relative decline in $V_1 + K_1$ is consistent with the rise in C_1/C_2.

Now as we approach the world of Tugan-Baranowsky where '. . . given a proportional distribution of social production, no decline in social consumption is capable of producing a superfluous product'.[65] Formally considered, all is well and accumulation can proceed to the point at which the output of sector II approaches zero: Indeed—'proportional distribution of social

[64] W. W. Rostow, *British Economy of the Nineteenth Century*, Oxford, 1948, pp. 38–42. However, since 1948 the minor cycle in the United States has reproduced itself at least four times. This does not invalidate Rostow's thesis but does suggest that other forces are currently operating, e.g. vast government expenditures help to maintain effective demand.

[65] M. Tugan-Baranowsky, *Studien zur Theorie and Geschichte der Handelskrisen in England* (1901). Quoted by Sweezy, *op. cit.*, p. 169.

production' accompanied by secular impoverishment and/or a rapid decrease in population!

Apart from the implications for population growth, there are two other objections to the thesis that accumulation can proceed to the point where the output of sector II approaches zero. First, suppose total net output were divided between sectors I and II as follows:

Net Value of I's Output is $800.00		Net Value of II's Output is $200.00	
Profits are	640.00	Profits are	160.00
Wages are	160.00	Wages are	40.00

Demand for I's Output is $800.00		Demand for II's Output is $200.00	
All of I's Profits	640.00	I's Wages	160.00
All of II's Profits	160.00	II's Wages	40.00

In this example, profits would be 80 per cent of national income and still the businessmen would be unable to consume! Should they consume, demand for the output of sector I would be inadequate. In other words, the thesis that accumulation can proceed indefinitely by investing in mills-to-make-more-mills fails, since investment would be interrupted by a profit shortage. Incidentally, Grossman proved in his polemic with Otto Bauer that even with a high rate of profit the amount of surplus value would be insufficient to maintain a given rate of accumulation.[66]

The second objection is based on the specificity of capital equipment:

J. B. Clark's picture of building 'mills to build more mills for ever' can never be actualized, since in the real world mills are always specialized to a particular current stream of demand connected with consumption in the near future, and not a stream of demand stretching to an infinite future.[67]

The requirement that investment in means of production ultimately must be justified explains, I believe, the apparent contradiction found in *Capital* that has been stressed by some writers: It will be recalled that Marx rejected under-consump-

[66] Henryk Grossman, *op. cit.*, p. 119.
[67] Maurice Dobb, *op. cit.*, p. 123.

tion as an explanation of crises—in particular, Marx took issue with Rodbertus by pointing out that 'crises are precisely always preceded by a period in which wages rise generally and the working class actually get a larger share of the annual product intended for consumption';[68] nevertheless, Marx also pointed out that

> The last cause of all real crises always remains the poverty and restricted consumption of the masses as compared to the tendency of capitalist production to develop the productive forces in such a way, that only the absolute power of consumption of the entire society would be their limit.[69]

Now, *cet. par.* a rise in wages (i.e. an increase in labour's share of national income) *would* increase workers' consumption and *would* diminish the mass of profits. This takes us back to the Ricardo-Malthus debate over accumulation. The dilemma is not rejected by Marx. On the contrary, the 'profit-consumption' (or cost-demand) dilemma is for Marx a fundamental contradiction for capitalism. Let us explore this contradiction in more detail.

Before proceeding with our exposition it is essential to dispose of a not infrequent misinterpretation of the Marxian analysis of cyclical phenomena, viz. the thesis that Marx had *not one but two explanations of the business cycle*. Thus Marx has been interpreted as at one time explaining cyclical behaviour as the consequence of sectoral disequilibrium and, at another time, as suggesting that depressions are caused by a profit squeeze consequent upon a wage rise resulting from a labour shortage.

I believe that those who have interpreted Marx as explaining crises as a consequence of a labour shortage have confused the Marxian analysis of primitive accumulation—mercantilism, which is characterized by a labour shortage—with the subsequent stage of industrial capitalism in which the labour shortage is eliminated. Thus, Sweezy in his chapter on 'Crises Associated with the Falling Rate of Profit' quotes Marx's statement that

> If the quantity of unpaid labour supplied by the working class,

---

[68] *Capital*, Vol. II, p. 476. 'A larger share of the annual product intended for consumption' is not, of course, a larger share of national income. For a discussion of real wages and labour's share see below, pp. 95 ff.

[69] *Ibid.*, Vol. III, p. 568.

and accumulated by the capitalist class, increases so rapidly that its conversion into capital requires an extraordinary addition of paid labour, then wages rise, and, all other circumstances remaining equal, the unpaid labour diminishes in proportion. But as soon as this diminution touches the point at which the surplus-labour that nourishes capital is no longer supplied in normal quantity, a reaction sets in: a smaller part of the revenue is capitalized, accumulation lags, and the movement of rise in wages receives a check.[70]

But this passage occurs in the section headed 'The Increased Demand for Labour-Power That Accompanies Accumulation, The Composition of Capital Remaining the Same', and hence *excludes accumulation under industrial capitalism*. Sweezy is on firmer ground in his other citation. In Volume III, Marx did consider an extreme case in which there would be an absolute overproduction of capital[71]—'absolute' in the sense that additional expenditures on labour-power would yield no additional surplus-value. In the extreme case assumed by Marx, the organic composition of capital could rise while, simultaneously, the growth of variable capital *might* exceed the growth of the labour force. In such a case, wages would rise and consequently interrupt the accumulation process. To repeat, Marx treated this as an 'extreme case'. Further, Marx did not develop this line of thought to imply that such an occurence was in any way *typical of the evolution of industrial capitalism*. When one considers the stress Marx placed on the creation of an industrial reserve army through the very process of accumulation, it seems more consistent with the Marxian analysis (and the empirical data) to hold that accumulation of industrial capital solves the labour shortage that was characteristic of primitive accumulation.[72]

Incidentally, indirect confirmation of the preceding thesis is given by the ideology of liberal capitalism. The ideologists of early nineteenth century capitalism could acquiesce in the legalization of trade unions and the elimination of laws estab-

[70] Paul Sweezy, *The Theory of Capitalist Development*, p. 150. The reference is to Volume I of *Capital*, p. 680.

[71] *Capital*, Vol. III, p. 295.

[72] It is obvious that a rise in wages, *cet. par.*, reduces profits. But the point is, are crises precipitated by wage increases in the period of industrial capitalism? To my knowledge there is no evidence to support this hypothesis.

lishing maximum wages, and could support, even enthusiastically, anti-slavery legislation, simply because industrial capitalism solved the labour shortage. In brief, the ideology of liberal capitalism had its economic rationale.

Marxian economic theory postulates a rise in the capital-labour ratio, i.e. sector I grows more rapidly than sector II. The implications are as follows: (1) *cet. par.*, a falling rate of profit and (2) a decrease in labour's share of national income. Such are the secular tendencies. The problem is to relate these secular tendencies to cyclical phenomena. First, however, it should be remarked that Marx acknowledges many offsets to the secular tendency of the rate of profit to fall. Further, the development of monopoly capitalism or oligopoly introduces another and very significant counter-tendency. The question, then, of a fall in the rate of profit cannot be resolved theoretically. The empirical data suggest that after 1919 the rate of exploitation in the United States rose sufficiently to maintain the rate of profit during the 1920s. The same appears true in the post-World War II period. But there is a difference in that monopolists now utilize state capitalism to maintain profits through accelerated depreciation allowances.

In what follows, then, we shall put aside the Marxian secular tendency for a fall in the rate of profit. What will be attempted is an integration of the secular tendency for labour's share in national income to fall with cyclical phenomena consequent upon sectoral disequilibrium.

Let us proceed on the basis of the following assumptions: (1) the overall capital-labour ratio is rising secularly, hence the output of the producer goods sector increases more rapidly than that of the consumer goods sector; (2) the ratio of C_1 to C_2 is crucial and, moreover, changes historically; (3) Kondratieff long-wave price changes are a valid description of English economic development.[73]

Now the price rise in the first phase of the first Kondratieff (1789–1814) reflected the Napoleonic Wars. Analytically, war expenditures (like gold mining) must be considered as similar to a growth of the producer goods sector in that the *immediate*

---

[73] Nikolai D. Kondratieff, 'The Long Waves in Economic Life' (an abridged translation by W. F. Stolper), *The Review of Economic Statistics*, Vol. XVII, No. 6, reprinted in *Readings in Business Cycle Theory*, pp. 20 ff.

effect is to augment the demand but not the supply of consumer goods. The ratio of C_1 to C_2 rises, hence the price rise during the period 1789–1814.

In the second long wave of the first Kondratieff (1815–45) the rate of increase of the producer goods sector continues to exceed that of the consumer goods sector. However, now the ratio of C_1 to C_2 falls. In this period, major economies in production are effected in the consumer sector which, in spite of its lower rate of increase of output, continues to constitute the bulk of total production. Hence the tendency for prices to fall. But, as has been suggested earlier, the tendency for prices to fall is aggravated by chronic overproduction of consumer goods, i.e. for dC_2 to exceed $dV_1 + dK_1$. Here, then, sector disequilibrium also operates to depress prices.

To achieve greater generality, it is necessary now to indicate how the disequilibrium characteristic of this period, over-investment in sector II, was determined by the process of capitalist accumulation. During the second wave of the first Kondratieff, or what, more properly, should be termed the *first phase of industrialization*, business typically suffered from a shortage of capital.[74] Such being the case, the tendency was to eschew long-term commitments. Investment sought out those areas in which the turn-over of capital was rapid and the quantity of capital required was minimal. Given a market economy, heavy investment in the producer goods sector must await accumulation in the consumer goods sector. In short, the delay in the mechanization of heavy industry appears not to be attributable to a lack of technological progress in this sector. Of course, technology is important but I would emphasize the quick gains to be achieved by limited investment in the consumer goods sector as the major cause of the technological lag in the producer goods sector. Or, if one prefers, the mechanization of the producer goods sector is subject to an 'accelerator principle' operating in the very long run.[75]

---

[74] According to H. L. Beales, in the text-books 'The first phase, from 1815 to 1846, has not acquired a generally accepted distinguishing label. . . .' ('The "Great Depression" in Industry and Trade', *The Economic History Review* October 1934, p. 65). As indicated above, in my view this period should be described as the first phase of capitalist industrialization, characterized by heavy investment in the consumer goods sector.

[75] cf. the previously quoted statement by Hoffmann, *supra*, p. 86.

Can we relate the sector disequilibrium characteristic of this period to Marx's secular tendency towards a decline in labour's share in national income? First, it is essential to recognize that *if productivity is increasing,* a rise in real wages is consistent with either a rise or fall in labour's share in national income. If, for example, real wages rise more than productivity increases, labour's share in national income rises. If, however, the rise in real wages is not proportional to productivity gains, labour's share in national income falls. A third possibility, of course, is that real wages fall although productivity is rising. In what follows, then, *the analysis proceeds on the basis of the distribution effects.* Further, overall changes in distribution will vary in their effects upon the producer and consumer goods sector. The analysis must proceed by isolating the sectoral impact of changes in demand and supply (cost).

Consider first the results of an overall increase in labour's share in national income. Demand for consumption goods must rise since we have assumed that workers of both sectors, unlike entrepreneurs, spend all of their income on consumption. Entrepreneurs in both departments will have rising costs. However, the rise in labour costs in the consumer goods sector will be more than compensated for by the proportionately greater increase in demand. On the other hand, a rise in wage costs in the producer goods sector is not offset by any immediate increase in demand for the output of this sector. In short, a rise in labour's share of national income increases demand more than costs in the consumer goods sector; whereas, in the producer goods sector, the rise in labour's share increases costs but not demand. Given competition, the effect will be for investment in labour-power to shift from the producer to the consumer goods sector. It is obvious that the sectoral impact of a rise in labour's share in national income will also depend upon the labour-capital ratios. If, as we have argued, during the first stage of industrialization, the labour-capital ratio is higher in the producer goods sector, then an increase of labour's share in national income means the capital goods sector sustains an even greater loss.

It was stated that a rise in labour's share in national income increases costs but not demand for the producer goods sector. But, it may be objected, a rise in wage costs would lead to the substitution of machinery for labour and hence an increased demand for the output of producer goods. But would such be the case? According to Ricardo:

> Every rise of wages . . . or, which is the same thing, every fall of profits, would lower the relative value of those commodities which were produced with a capital of a durable nature and would proportionally elevate those which were produced with capital more perishable. A fall in wages would have precisely the contrary effect. [76]

Ricardo also contended that a rise in wages would lead to the substitution of machinery for labour. In his analysis, Ricardo assumed that some fixed capital was used to produce machinery but none to produce labour-power. But was such an assumption legitimate? In the Ricardian analysis, the value of labour-power equals the cost of subsistence of the workers. If then, wage-goods rise relative to the price of machinery must not the value of labour-power also rise relative to machinery? In the following table, we assume that *the capital-labour ratio in the wage-goods sector is the same as that of the consumer goods sector*. Then, on our assumption that the consumer goods sector is more capital intensive, the value of labour-power falls relative to machinery.

Prior to a Wage Rise	Capital	Labour	Surplus	Value of Output $(C+L+S)$	Prices of Production $(C+L)(p'^*+1)$
Machinery	4	6	6	16	15
Gold†	3	3	3	9	9
Wage-Goods	6	4	4	14	15
After a 50% Wage Rise					
Machinery	4	9	3	16	15·60
Gold†	3	4·5	1·5	9	9
Wage-Goods	6	6	2	14	14·40

$*p'$ = the average rate of profit, i.e. the ratio of total surplus value to the total outlays on capital and labour, $S/C + L$.

† A commodity whose inputs are assumed to correspond to the average capital-labour ratio in production.

---

[76] *Principles of Political Economy and Taxation, op. cit.*, pp. 39–40.

Socialists and Dissidents

In the above example, the rate of profit fell from 50 per cent to 20 per cent, and the price of machinery rose relative to labour-power. We arrive at the apparently paradoxical conclusion that a rise in labour's share in national income, during the first period of industrialization *cet. par.* leads to a reduced demand for producer goods.

Consider now an overall decrease in labour's share in national income, which (to repeat) may or may not be accompanied by a rise or fall in real wages. In this case, as would be expected, the results are opposite to those derived on the assumption of a rise in labour's share. Costs will fall in the consumer goods sector but the demand for consumer goods will fall even more. In the producer goods sector, however, costs will fall but not demand. Potential demand for producer goods is increased by the rise in the share of entrepreneurial income. But, more significantly, given the assumption of a higher labour-capital ratio in the producer goods sector, the reduction in wage costs will induce the substitution of machinery for labour by the consumer goods sector. Again, we reach an apparently paradoxical conclusion: *viz. the demand for labour varies directly and not inversely with labour's share in national income.*

Generalizations on the Sectoral Impact of Changes in Distribution

The preceding discussion was oriented to the first and second phases of industrialization. More generally, the sectoral impact of changes in distribution on price-cost ratios and factor utilization is shown in the table on the following page.

The table is constructed from our previous assumptions, viz. (1) only two classes exist in society; (2) workers spend all of their income on consumption; (3) therefore, all saving (investment) is performed by entrepreneurs. Because we have divided *net* national product into two integrated sectors and assumed specific capital-labour ratios characteristic of each sector, it follows that changes in distribution between capital and labour do not result in any substitution between capital and labour *within sector I*, the producer of capital goods. This, of course, is to oversimplify; nevertheless, the abstraction facilitates, I believe, without distorting the analysis. Consequently, as is shown in column 7 of the table, the effect of an

97

Primary and Secondary Sectoral Effects of Changes in Distribution on Price-Cost Ratios (Profits) and Factor Utilization Given Different Capital-Labour Ratios*

Possibilities (1)	Labour's Share in National Income (2)	Direct Effect on Price-Cost Ratio For		Factor Utilization		Secondary Effect or Changes in Demand for Capital by II (7)
		I (3)	II (4)	Labour Intensive (5)	Capital Intensive (6)	
A	rises	−	+	I	II	−
B	falls	+	−	I	II	+
C	rises	−	+	II	I	+
D	falls	+	−	II	I	−

* As before, we assume the capital-labour ratio in the consumer goods sector is the capital-labour ratio for the wage-goods industry.

overall change in distribution on the demand for capital is given by changes in the demand for capital goods by the consumer goods sector.

The table demonstrates that an increase in labour's share in national income is always detrimental to the capital goods sector. The direct effect is to increase costs but not demand for capital goods. If we postulate an economy governed by Say's Law of Markets, i.e. no interruption of the accumulation process, the secondary effects may either aggravate or meliorate the unfavourable price-cost ratio (profit-squeeze) in I. If the capital goods sector is labour intensive (possibility A in the table), a rise in labour's share in national income not only reduces the entrepreneurial 'fund' available for investment in fixed capital but also the relative demand for capital goods by II—i.e. the tendency will be for II to substitute labour for capital.[77] If, however, the capital goods sector were less labour intensive than the consumer goods sector (possibility C in the table), a rise in labour's share in national income would increase the demand for capital goods *vis à vis* labour—i.e. sector II would tend to substitute capital for labour. It was this substitution effect that Ricardo had in mind when he assumed that some fixed capital was used to produce machinery but none to produce labour-power. We have argued that fixed capital is used to produce both machinery and labour-power; nevertheless, given that the producer sector is more capital intensive, we obtain the same result. However, in the Ricardian analysis, the substitution of capital for labour is the compensating mechanism which relieves the profit squeeze consequent upon a wage rise.

But Ricardo's compensating mechanism would not prevail. Rather—and this Ricardo ignored because of his acceptance of Say's Law of Markets—a crisis would ensue because of the profit-squeeze in I.[78] Output of investment goods, the strategic variable for prosperity, would be curtailed. Unemployment in the capital goods sector would decrease the demand for consumer goods. In short, a cyclical fall in the mass of profit

[77] '. . . there is on the average about twice as much labour in capital goods as in consumption goods.' *Capital Goods and the American Enterprise System*, Machinery and Allied Products Institute, Chicago, April 1939, p. 38.

[78] As Marx would say, modern advocates of a high consumption economy please take note!

consequent upon a shift in distribution to labour is, in essence, a decline in profits for the capital goods sector. Output and employment in the capital goods sector are reduced. The consequent fall in demand for consumer goods appears as over-production in II. The Marxian profit-consumption dilemma (the Ricardo-Malthus controversy), or the truism that wages are both costs and demand, is most clearly evident by disaggregating output into consumer and producer goods sectors.

Given a rise in labour's share in national income, the preceding analysis shows how it is possible to integrate the Marxian analysis of distribution with sectoral disequilibrium. A rise in labour's share in national income adversely affects the capital goods sector. Conversely, a shift in distribution favourable to entrepreneurs benefits the producer goods sector. The immediate impact is a fall in costs but not demand. On the other hand, the fall of labour's share in national income reduces demand more than costs for the consumer sector. Only if entrepreneurs of both sectors increase their consumption expenditures sufficiently to compensate for the workers' reduced demand for consumer goods, can the consumer goods sector benefit from a shift in distribution favourable to capital. But this is not a realistic hypothesis.

Incidentally, the tendency for real wages to fall during prosperity has been utilized by Hayek to explain the business cycle.[79] Ricardo had argued that a rise in real wages would lead to the substitution of capital for labour. Conversely, and this is Hayek's point, a fall in real wages induces the substitution of labour for machinery, a shortening of the period of production. As the boom progresses, prices rise more than money wages. The decline in real wages reduces the demand for capital goods and thus precipitates a crisis.

Concerning Hayek's analysis, the following points are relevant: (1) Alvin Hansen rejects Hayek's analysis on the grounds that the data available indicate that real wages rise during prosperity.[80] But, as has been shown, Hansen misses

---

[79] Frederick Hayek, *Profits, Interest and Investment*, London, 1939, first essay.

[80] Alvin Hansen, *Business Cycles and National Income*, New York, 1951, p. 392. Hansen does, however, go on to point out that the substitution of machinery for labour is determined by 'the money wage rate in relation to the price of machinery, assuming no changes in technology or the personal efficiency of the worker'. (*Ibid.*, p. 392.) No doubt!

the point since a rise in real wages is consistent with a decrease in labour's share of national income. (2) In developing his thesis, Ricardo assumed fixed capital was utilized for the production of machinery but not for wage-goods.[81] On this assumption, given Say's Law of Markets, Ricardo was obviously correct.

Superficially, it might appear that Hayek's explanation of the business cycle would be valid if (1) labour's share in national income falls,[82] and (2) production in the capital goods sector is less labour-intensive than in the consumer goods sector, in which case costs in the consumer sector fall more than in the producer goods sector. But this will not do because the fall in labour's share in national income reduces demand more than costs for the consumer sector. A fall in labour's share of national income benefits the capital sector at the expense of the consumer sector. *If* a fall in real wages should precipitate a depression, the crisis would originate in the consumer sector, *not in the producer goods sector.* Subsequently, of course, the profit-squeeze in the consumer sector will reduce the demand for capital goods.

Cet. par., a shift in distribution favourable to capital increases profits in the producer goods sector at the expense of profits in the consumer sector. Contraction of output in the consumer goods sector, in turn, reduces demand for capital goods; i.e. *relative over-production of consumer goods may culminate in general over-production.* Relative over-production of consumer goods will precipitate a *general crisis* if, as assumed in our table, all changes in demand for capital goods originate in II and are attributable to changes in distribution.

However, let us depart from the assumptions of our table and introduce a concept akin to what modern economists term 'autonomous' investment: i.e. investment within sector I independent of changes in demand for capital goods by the consumer goods sector consequent upon relative changes in the price of capital goods. In this case, increased profits in I

---

[81] David Ricardo, *On the Principles of Political Economy and Taxation, op. cit.*, pp. 40–1.

[82] '. . . Hayek could argue that for his theory it is really the rate of profit and not real wages that matter. Even if real wages rise in the upswing, profits may rise too.' Gottfried Haberler, *Prosperity and Depression* (third edition), New York, 1946, p. 491.

may result in accelerated investment in fixed capital within sector I. That is, if a shift in distribution favourable to property income occurs during the second stage of industrialization when C_1/C_2 is rising, heavy investment in the producer goods sector may mitigate or obviate the effect of a decreased demand for capital goods by the consumer sector.

But, it may be objected, if we drop our assumption of all changes in demand for capital originating in II as a consequence of relative changes in the price of capital goods, must we not also consider 'autonomous' investment by the producers of consumer goods? Assume, then, 'autonomous' investment by both sectors. Nevertheless, given an increase in property's share, the consumer sector remains subject to a constraint more powerful than that operating in the producer goods sector. The profit-squeeze in II reduces the 'fund' for 'autonomous' investment in II. Further, the chances that such investment will turn out to be justified are reduced by the proportionately greater decrease in demand than costs in II. *En passant*, the possibility just considered is strategic for the analysis of the thirties in the United States. Subsequently, we shall utilize this model to explain 'The Great Depression'.

Alternatively, given 'autonomous' investment in II coupled with a shift in distribution to labour, the consumer sector profits at the expense of the capital sector. True, a secular boom in the capital goods industries, C_1/C_2 rises, could offset the profit-squeeze in I consequent upon a rise in labour's share in national income. But, *cet. par.*, a secular boom in the capital sector will negate the rise in labour's share. Demand for consumer goods will increase more than supply, thus reducing labour's share: i.e. consumption as a per cent of gross national product falls. In short, a secular boom in the capital goods sector is facilitated by the shift in distribution to property, which the boom itself engenders.

Our distinction between 'autonomous' investment and investment 'induced' by changes in factor prices differs from that employed in current economic writings. In contemporary analysis, 'induced' investment abstracts from changes in factor prices. Instead, 'induced' investment is defined as investment resulting from increases in output either in the producer or consumer sector, i.e., the familiar acceleration principle. Our

102

justification for ignoring the accelerator principle is as follows:

> Are cyclical fluctuations in investment actually induced by current or prior changes in consumption or total output in any clearly observable way? The factual evidence is virtually all in the negative. Whatever value the acceleration principle may have as an explanation of certain long-run relationships, it seems of limited value in explaining short-run fluctuations in investment.[83]

Cet. par., a shift in distribution to labour constitutes a shift to profits for the consumer sector. Conversely, the same phenomenon constitutes a profit-squeeze for the producer goods sector, the magnitude of which depends on the capital-labour ratio in this sector. Interestingly, the beneficial effect of a shift in distribution to labour for the consumer goods sector finds empirical confirmation in the following:

> From its beginning the 'New Deal' was underwritten by those wealthy individuals whose revenues derive primarily from direct exploitation of the retail market—department-store owners, textile fabricators, cigarette manufacturers, independent industrialists, processors and distributors, and big real-estate operators. Excepting the latter, these comprise the light industries group. And because the task of the 'New Deal' was to restore prosperity to these beleaguered capitalists by restoring purchasing power to the populace, it succeeded in rallying around itself organized labour and the farmers; for in expanding popular purchasing power certain immediate small benefits accrued to these latter. . . . The light goods industrialists and merchants . . . were quick to take advantage of Hoover's unpopularity to install the 'New Deal', espousing policies for which

---

[83] Robert Aaron Gordon, *Business Fluctuations*, New York, 1952, p. 112. cf. also Gottfried Haberler, *op. cit.*, pp. 96 ff. The difficulty is that typically business has excess capacity. However, in rejecting the acceleration principle we do not mean to deny *any* interaction between investment and consumption. In moving from depression to prosperity, increased investment will increase consumption which, in turn, may increase the demand for investment by the consumer sector. Increased demand may be anticipated by the consumer sector and hence the difficulty of demonstrating the acceleration principle. Nevertheless, to speak of changes in output inducing investment places the wrong emphasis, in that changes in output are basically the result of changes in investment. Again, from an historical point of view, the tendency to capital saturation, i.e. excess capacity, suggests a secular attenuation of the contribution of the accelerator to changes in output.

the Democratic Party has always more or less stood. So-called economic reforms under the 'New Deal' have all, it is pertinent to observe, been engineered at the expense of the big banks and the heavy industries. The 1936 measure taxing corporate surpluses, for example, was directed only at the heavy industries and banks, which had built up big surpluses in the 1920s and had preserved them by dropping millions of workmen from their payrolls during the depression. The discharge of these millions and their consequent loss of purchasing power had the effect of cutting into the surpluses of the light industries, consisting in the main of inventories which had to be turned over several times annually in order for profits to be made. The 'New Deal' light industrialists, to protect themselves against a recurrence of such destruction of the retail market by general layoffs throughout heavy industry, have encouraged the unionization programme of John L. Lewis and the Committee for Industrial Organization. This programme has been directed to date only against the citadels of heavy industry—steel, oil, chemicals, coal, and automobiles—and although the C.I.O. will in time probably take light industry under its jurisdiction this will be a matter of little concern to light industrialists secure in the knowledge that the employment policy of heavy industry is locked in a vice.[84]

A market economy has a bias against an increase in labour's share of national income. And because of the profit-consumption dilemma, a decrease in labour's share can precipitate a crisis originating in the consumer sector. But of the two alternatives, capitalism more easily can tolerate a fall in labour's share in national income. The consumer goods sector can be sacrificed, given either a boom in the producer sector or, as is now the case, increased government expenditures on armaments, which in the United States have reduced consumption as a percentage of gross national product by approximately

[84] Ferdinand Lundberg, *America's Sixty Families* (New York, 1937), reprinted by Citadel Press, New York, 1960, pp. 450–2. According to Lundberg, 'The automobile industry does not . . . really belong to the retail market. It cannot, for example, sell its product over-the-counter for cash; it must finance its essentially uneconomic sales by means of an elaborate instalment system that utilizes a great amount of bank credit. Furthermore, it is closely bound in with heavy industry in that it is one of the hungriest outlets for steel, copper, nickel and chemicals. The automobile industry, in short, belongs to heavy industry and finance capital.' (*Ibid.*, p. 487).

15 per cent, comparing 1928 with the 1950s.[85] However, in the absence of vast government expenditures, and given the fact that investment in the producer sector can achieve only temporary independence from consumption, changes in distribution disrupt the precarious balance between the producer and consumer sectors. Here, then, is the explanation of the so-called constancy of shares of labour and capital in distribution. It must not be forgotten, however, 'that this constancy does not hold true on a year-to-year basis; that at best it can be said to hold true only on a cycle-to-cycle basis, and, finally, that the data . . . cover only the years since 1919, the period of rapidly maturing world capitalism'.[86]

Our problem was to relate Marx's theory of a secular decline in labour's share in national income with the cyclical phenomena consequent upon sectoral disequilibrium. We saw that Marx was impatient with under-consumptionist prescriptions. Nevertheless, Marx asserted 'the last cause of all real crises'— was the restricted purchasing power of the people. Again, Marx recognized that prior to crises, real wages rose. To resolve the apparent contradiction, it was necessary to distinguish between changes in real wages and distribution. Here Marx's formulation (the rough notes comprising volumes II and III out of which Engels was 'to make something') was inadequate and, moreover, failed to do justice to Marx's own emphasis upon the multiplication of use-values consequent upon accumulation. However, by concentrating upon changes in distribution it was possible to reconcile the apparent contradiction. An increase in labour's share of national income, the under-consumptionist's panacea, increases profits in the consumer sector but reduces entrepreneurial outlays in the producer goods sector. The reduction of entrepreneurial outlays in the producer sector results in over-production of consumer goods.

How, then, is underconsumption 'the last cause of all real

---

[85] One must not overlook the possibility of a *temporary* rise in labour's share of national income although consumption as a percentage of gross national product falls. In a modified market economy (the so-called mixed economy) taxation policies can be such as to redistribute the gains from the consumer sector to the producer goods sector: i.e. the rise in labour's share in national income, which would, *cet. par.*, benefit entrepreneurs in the consumer sector, can be negated through government policy.

[86] Joseph M. Gillman, *The Falling Rate of Profit*, London, 1957, p. 153.

crises'? In the Marxian model the rise in the organic composition of capital, *cet. par.*, results in a fall in labour's share in national income. The rise in the capital-labour ratio is both a secular and a cylical phenomenon which is subject, of course, to counter-tendencies, e.g. the write-down of fixed capital values through depression. The preceding analysis considered changes in capital-labour ratios as induced by changes in distribution. But substitution of capital for labour obviously is not limited to changes in distribution. Given no change in distribution, technological developments may be such as to reduce costs by substituting capital for labour:

> The use of machinery for the exclusive purpose of cheapening the product, is limited in this way, that less labour must be expended in producing the machinery than is displaced by the employment of that machinery. For the capitalist, however, this use is still more limited. Instead of paying for the labour, he only pays the value of the labour-power employed; therefore, the limit to his using a machine is fixed by the difference between the value of the machine and the value of the labour-power replaced by it.[87]

Apart from Marx's formal model, it appears that in the early stages of industrialization, labour's share in national income fell, i.e. the major gains from productivity went to the entrepreneurial class.[88] Now in the absence of a secular boom in the capital goods sector during which investment achieves temporary independence from consumption, a fall in labour's share in national income precipitates a crisis originating in the consumer goods sector and culminating in general overproduction. As has been emphasized, a market economy is biased against an increase in labour's share in national income. It is in this sense that under-consumption constitutes 'the last cause of all real crises'.

[87] *Capital*, Vol. I, pp. 428–9. In a footnote to this passage Marx wrote: 'Hence in a communistic society there would be a very different scope for the employment of machinery than there can be in a bourgeois society.'

[88] Gladstone stated in the House of Commons (Feb. 13, 1843): 'It is one of the most melancholy features in the social state of this country that we see, beyond the possibility of denial, that while there is at this moment a decrease in the consuming powers of the people . . . there is at the same time a constant accumulation of wealth in the upper classes, an increase of the luxuriousness of their habits, and of their means of enjoyment.' Quoted by Marx, *Capital*, Vol. I, p. 715, n. 2.

The preceding exposition of the Marxian analysis shows how it is possible to integrate both secular and cyclical phenomena. Given the general law of capitalist accumulation, i.e. that the output of the producer goods sector must grow more rapidly than that of the consumer sector, the strategic variable is historic changes in the ratio of C_1 to C_2. Thus, in the first phase of capitalist industrialization (1814–c. 1845) the overall rise in the capital-labour ratio is attributable to greater investment in fixed capital in the consumer sector. Given a market economy, entrepreneurs cultivate those areas in which the turn-over of capital is rapid and the quantity required minimal. This secular pattern of accumulation explains the falling price level. Again, this secular pattern of accumulation determines cyclical phenomena, i.e. the chronic tendency to over-production of consumer goods, which is aggravated by a decline in labour's share in national income. The (temporary) restoration of the equilibrium condition for balanced growth, $dC_2 = dV_1 + dK_1$, is achieved through short, minor cycles of approximately four years duration. It should also be noted that cyclical over-production of consumer goods reinforces the secular tendency for prices to fall consequent upon the pattern of accumulation.

In the second stage of capitalist industrialization (c. 1846–73), a rise in the C_1–C_2 ratio occurs. Mechanization of the producer goods sector permits investment to become for a time independent of consumption. Heavy investment in the consumer sector during the preceding period makes feasible (justifies) heavy investment in the producer sector in the subsequent period. (Or, if we prefer, we may term the subsequent heavy investment in fixed capital in the producer sector as the operation of a long-run accelerator principle. Nevertheless, if we confine our attention to the second period, investment in the producer goods sector may be considered as 'autonomous'.) The greatly increased share of producer goods in total output reverses the preceding secular fall in prices: i.e. demand for consumer goods increases more than supply. The discovery of gold in Australia and California further intensified the price rise. As previously noted, for an understanding of price phenomena, production of gold, like armaments, is an extreme case of the production of producer goods—'extreme' in the sense that such 'producer goods' greatly increase the demand but, at best, only indirectly augment somewhat the supply of consumer goods. Again, the greatly increased share of producer goods in total output changes the duration of the business cycle, viz. gradual elimination (subject, of course, to exceptions) of the short, minor cycles of over-production. The seven- to ten-year cycle, possibly connected with the life of fixed capital (as Marx suggested), becomes predominant.[89]

Is it possible to analyse the third stage of capitalist industrialization in Great Britain (1873–96) in terms of changes in the ratio of C_1 to C_2? Our data on 'The Great Depression' are limited and the writer is not aware of any studies that allocate the output of sector I between sectors I and II. We have, however, the following suggestive findings: (1) The average annual rate of growth of industrial output declined from 3·2 to 1·7 per cent or by approximately 46 per cent.[90] (2) It was a period of falling prices. (3) Contrary to Rostow, the decline in foreign lending was *not* 'the central causal force in the Great Depression'.[91] It was 'a period of "lean years" in contrast with the preceding good years, if profits were the main criterion of welfare'.[92]

The sharp decline in the rate of growth of industrial output suggests that the period of independence of investment from consumption ended in 1873. Over-production and the fall in prices has been attributed by students of the period to increased productivity and foreign competition.[93] In terms of our model, the fall in prices and decline in the rate of growth of industrial

[89] A recent work explains the nine-year cycles in England during the period 1790–1850 as a result of the 'bunching' of investment. 'Bunching' occurred because investment was dependent upon accumulated profits and, also, 'investment in new plant could not, of its nature, be undertaken in small increments'. A. Gayer, W. W. Rostow and A. J. Schwartz, *The Growth and Fluctuation of the British Economy* 1790–1850, Oxford, 1953, Vol. II, p. 554. Given that investment was a function of past profits, and given a tendency to chronic over-production of consumer goods, then *cet. par.* the secular rate of growth of a market economy must be less than that of a planned economy during the initial period of industrialization.

[90] Walter Hoffmann, 'Ein Index der Industriellen Producktion', *Weltwirschaftliches Archiv*, 1934, cited by Rostow, *op. cit.*, p. 8.

[91] *Op. cit.*, p. 88. For a criticism of Rostow's thesis see Brinley Thomas, *Migration and Economic Growth*, Cambridge, 1954, p. 188, n. 1.

[92] H. L. Beales, 'The "Great Depression" in Industry and Trade', *Economic History Review*, October 1934, p. 75.

[93] i.e. not to a shortage of gold and silver. See in particular David A. Wells, *Recent Economic Changes*, New York, 1895.

output means that the dominant tendency of the first phase of industrialization recurs, i.e. a chronic tendency for C_2 to exceed $V_1 + K_1$. But the essential difference between the first and third period of industrialization is obscured by the preceding equation. In the first period, the average annual rate of growth of industrial output was 3·5 per cent; whereas, in the third phase, the rate of growth was a mere 1·7 per cent. In other words, during the first phase of capitalist industrialization, disequilibrium must be attributed to over-investment in the consumer sector; whereas, in the third phase it would be more apt to attribute disequilibrium to stagnation in the producer goods sector, i.e. a relative reduction of entrepreneurial expenditures by sector I on labour and consumption:

> For over thirty years the main investment effort in Britain had been concentrated on railways, but by 1875 most of the main-line railways were already in being, and from then on railway-building normally absorbed smaller amounts of capital and, what was more important, a smaller proportion of new capital . . . industrial capital was still relatively small. Fixed capital in manufacturing was less in 1875 than the capital of the railways. It was transport and commerce that used large amounts of capital, not industry. In cotton, for example, the amount of capital employed was about 100 m. Yet at that time the cotton textile industry employed half a million workers, provided one-third of British exports, and was much the largest manufacturing industry. Even a rapid rate of growth in industrial capital, therefore, could not, starting from so narrow a base, readily take up the slack, when railway-building eased off.[94]

Excess capacity in the capital goods sector was aggravated by technological unemployment in specific industries in both the consumer and producer goods sectors.[95] Nevertheless, such data as are available do not indicate that unemployment was greater during the third phase of capitalist industrialization. It appears that the slow rate of economic advance characteristic of the first 'Great Depression' was sustained largely by investment in the consumer goods sector. Thus, between 1873 and 1883 about 400 new cotton companies were floated. Residential

[94] A. K. Cairncross, *Home and Foreign Investment* 1870–1913, Cambridge, 1953, pp. 8–9.
[95] David A. Wells, *op. cit.*, Ch. III.

construction was maintained, 'the number of houses in course of erection was almost exactly the same in 1871, 1891 and 1911'.[96] New shipbuilding for the Atlantic passenger trade and the frozen-meat industry was an important investment outlet. On the other hand, progress in the capital goods industry must not be ignored:

> In 1873 Bessemer steel in England, where its price has not been enhanced by protective duties, commanded $80 per ton; in 1886 it was profitably manufactured and sold in the same country for less than $20 per ton.[97]

Further, expenditures by local authorities increased from 92·82 £ million in 1874–5 to 234·48 £ million in 1894–5, the bulk of which was for the building of schools and for sanitary improvements.[98] On balance it seems probable the slow rate of economic advance was sustained by investment in the consumer sector and government expenditures.

Subsequent secular price changes, as well as other economic phenomena, can be interpreted in terms of changes in the C_1–C_2 ratio. Thus, what Schumpeter termed the 'Neomercantilist Kondratieff' (1898–1913) was characterized by a rapid development of electricity. More significantly, 'English and German war budgets—for all budgets from 1899 on were to all intents and purposes war budgets and the World War could have been, and to the knowledge of the writer actually has been, at least in one instance, predicted from their figures alone . . .'[99] raised the C_1/C_2. Again, the demise of competitive capitalism was marked by the export of capital goods, which, in turn, increased demand more than supply of consumer goods in the home market. Subsequently, curtailed war expenditures and the boom in consumer goods during the 1920s constituted a fall in the C_1/C_2.

The morphology of growth of an industrial market economy can be summarized as follows: An initial period of industrialization in which investment is directed into the consumer goods sector. A subsequent period characterized by the mechanization

[96] A. K. Cairncross, *op. cit.*, p. 147.
[97] David A. Wells, *op. cit.*, p. 43.
[98] A. K. Cairncross, *op. cit.*, pp. 143–4.
[99] Joseph A. Schumpeter, *Business Cycles*, New York and London, 1939. Vol. I, p. 400.

of the producer sector—or what we have termed the operation of a long-run accelerator principle. Here investment achieves temporary independence of consumption. A third stage in which the ratio of output of consumer to producer goods falls to about 2·5:1. The secular boom in the producer sector comes to an end. Stagnation tendencies, or at least a marked decline in the rate of economic growth occurs. The slow rate of economic advance is maintained largely by investment in the consumer sector. This critical point in the evolution of capitalism is superseded by Neomercantilism. The characteristic phenomena of Neomercantilism are excess capacity leading to cartel agreements on prices and production quotas, protectionism and government price supports, the export of capital, and most important of all, the militarization of the economy. State capitalism operates episodically to raise the C_1–C_2 ratio. 'Episodically' in that between World Wars I and II, government expenditures were for a time curtailed, particularly during the 1920s.[100]

The Marxian analysis did not anticipate the militarization of capitalism in its monopoly stage. Nor would Marx have agreed that the profit-consumption dilemma could be avoided through the proliferation of unproductive expenditures. Marx, like Marshall, believed that in the long run, wages approximate the cost of labour-power. Hence, the burden of unproductive expenditures could be only temporarily shifted to labour.

Lenin emphasized the importance of unproductive expenditures, specifically military, in his analysis of imperialism.

[100] Germany, however, constituted an exception: 'In 1925 the total expenditures of the federal government, the states, and the municipalities, including social insurance and reparations payments, amounted to . . . about 31·9 per cent of the national income as compared to . . . 18·9 per cent (post-war territory) in 1913.' Schumpeter, *op. cit.*, Vol. II, p. 717. Expenditures continued to rise through 1929. 'Analysis of the expenditure . . . undoubtedly reveals cultural and economic achievement, eminently productive of economic and supereconomic values . . . there is much to be set, in terms of beauty as well as in terms of welfare, against the desperate financial position into which the big cities manoeuvred themselves. But neither that cultural aspect nor the various deficits as such are pertinent to our subject. The important thing is the unavoidable inference that we have here a case of an excess of consumption by public bodies, inducing excesses all over the economic system, withdrawing capital from industry, or preventing its being built up—directly by taxation, indirectly by the ensuing rise in costs—and another illustration of the Doctrine of Spending.' *Ibid.*, pp. 717–18. In short, Schumpeter remained sceptical of the Keynesian panacea.

Military expenditures to obtain or retain colonies were necessary overhead costs of imperialism. Such expenditures might temporarily resolve the profit-consumption dilemma. But inevitably imperialism generates wars and revolutions.

In summary, Marx appears to remain formally in the classical tradition by defining productive labour as labour-power that yields a surplus, that is, labour-power that exchanges with capital. But not all capital. Some labour-power exchanges with merchant capital. Such labour is necessary for the realization of surplus-value. But circulation creates no value. Further consideration of the conditions necessary for the realization of surplus-value led Marx to develop a two-departmental scheme for the analysis of reproduction. In our exposition of the Marxian analysis we arrived at the following conclusions:

(1) The morphology of capitalist accumulation determines secular and cyclical phenomena.

(2) The profit-consumption dilemma is most clearly evident from the opposite effects of changes in distribution upon the capital and consumer sectors.

(3) Capitalism has an inherent bias against a shift in distribution favourable to labour because of its adverse effect on the capital goods sector. This bias stems from the basic law of accumulation, the rise in the capital-labour ratio, which requires that the producer goods sector grows more rapidly than the consumer goods sector.

(4) If the overall rise in the capital-labour ratio results from a more rapid rate of growth of C_2 than C_1, the equilibrium growth condition requires that V_1 (or $V_1 + K_1$) grow more rapidly than V_2 (or $V_2 + K_2$).

(5) Given a secular boom in the capital goods sector, capital can more easily tolerate a decline in labour's share of national income, i.e. the realization problem can be postponed.

(6) Nevertheless, given a boom in the capital goods sector, the realization problem cannot be indefinitely postponed since ultimately a point is reached where profits are insufficient to purchase the output of the producer goods sector.

(7) In the absence of a boom in the producer goods sector, the rise in the capital-labour ratio and the concomittant fall in labour's share in national income precipitates a crisis of over-production in the consumer sector.

Socialists and Dissidents

(8) Thus, the dilemma of capitalist accumulation: Either insufficient profits to continue the process of investment; or, given a boom in the consumer sector, the fall in labour's share of national income during prosperity precipitates a crisis of over-production in the consumer sector.

IV

ANTI-CLASSICAL THEORIES IN THE TWENTIETH CENTURY

THE MORPHOLOGY OF GROWTH of an industrial capitalist economy culminates in capital saturation. Given the profit-consumption dilemma (productive versus unproductive labour) an industrial capitalist economy finally reaches a stage in accumulation characterized by an absolute over-production of capital goods —'absolute' in the sense that existing capital cannot be profitably employed, given the institutional setting. Such, at least, is the Marx-Leninist analysis.

To a surprising degree anti-Classical writers either explicitly or implicitly accept the Marxian diagnosis but not, of course, the prescription. Whereas for Marx, the profit-consumption dilemma could be resolved only by abolishing the capitalist mode of production and substituting a social order based on production for use rather than profit, anti-Classical theorists of the twentieth century believe it possible to resolve the dilemma by modifying, but not abolishing, capitalism. The analysis, the means and the programmes differentiate contemporary critics into three camps: (1) all-out state capitalism, mobilized for war, i.e. fascism; (2) regulated capitalism (as in contemporary France) where government enters into a partnership with the business community, but leaves intact the basic social relations;[1] (3) Keynesian economics, which relies primarily on government fiscal and monetary policy for the achievement of full employment. In what follows, we discuss the Fascist (Nazi) and Keynesian theories of productive labour and effective demand.

[1] cf. A. Pokrovsky, 'The Essence of *Dirigisme* in Present-Day Bourgeois Political Economy in France' in *Theories of Regulated Capitalism*, Foreign Languages Publishing House, Moscow, (n.d.), pp. 163 ff.

114

Anti-Classical Theories in the Twentieth Century

(A) THE FASCIST SOLUTION

It is not our purpose to give a detailed analysis of the roots of Fascist ideology. We are interested, however, in relating certain aspects of this ideology to the distinction between productive and unproductive labour. Specifically, we have in mind the economic rationale that provided the justification for the apparently absurd identification of international bankers ('Jews') with world communism.

The roots of Nazi ideology can be found in the writings of Frederick List. In the mid-nineteenth century, List had objected to the Classical School's distinction between productive and unproductive labour because these economists had failed to appreciate the necessity of developing a nation's productive powers. Confounding private with public interest, Classical economics was defective in three essentials since it advocated firstly

> a chimerical *cosmopolitism*, which does not comprehend nationality, and which has no regard for national interests; secondly, a dead *materialism*, which regards everywhere the exchangeable value of things, taking account neither of the moral nor of the political interests of the present nor of the future, nor of the productive power of the nation; thirdly, a *separatism*, a disorganizing *individualism*. . . . But between the individual and the whole human race there is the nation with its special language and literature, with its own origin and history, with its manners and habits, its laws and institutions; with its claims to existence, its independence, its progress, its duration, and with its distinct territory; an association having not only an entirely separate existence, but having an intelligence and interest peculiarly its own, a whole existing for itself, acknowledging within itself the authority of the law, but claiming and enjoying full exemption from the control of the world, able to maintain its independence only by its own strength and proper resources.[2]

Again, the motto of the Classical economists, '*Laissez faire, laissez passer*', is

> not less suitable to highwaymen, knaves, and swindlers, than to merchants, and which, for that very reason, should be regarded with suspicion. That insane doctrine which sacrifices the interests of agriculture and manufacturing industry to the pre-

[2] Frederick List, *The National System of Political Economy*, pp. 262–3.

115

tensions of commerce—to the claims of absolute free trade, is the natural offspring of a theory too fully preoccupied with values, and too little with productive power, and which regards the whole world as simply a republic of merchants, one and indivisible.

The School does not perceive that the merchants can attain their object, which is wealth, by profits upon the commodities which pass through their hands even at the expense of agriculture and manufactures, at the expense of productive power, nay, even at the expense of national independence. . . . They deal in poisons as readily as medicines. . . . It is no concern for them whether their goods were legally imported or were smuggled, whether their business brings employment with bread to hundreds of thousands, or millions, or reduces as many to beggary, provided only the regular profit is realized.[3]

List had also provided the justification for racial imperialism:

The ruling section of the peoples of this earth has for some time been segregating itself according to descent. . . . One speaks of a German, a Romanic, a Slavonic race in a political aspect. This distinction alone seems destined to exercise great influence upon the practical politics of the future. At the head of the three races stand England, France, and Russia. . . . There is hardly any doubt that the Germanic race has, by virtue of its nature and character, been preferentially selected by Providence for the solution of the great task—to lead the affairs of the world, to civilize the wild barbaric countries, to populate those still uninhabited, for none of the others has the capacity to emigrate *en masse* and to found more perfect communities in foreign lands . . . and to keep free of the influences of barbaric and semi-barbaric aborigines.[4]

As Neumann puts it, List believed that

England inhabited by a Germanic race and equipped with a mighty fleet and vast empire, has the mission of reorganizing the world. But she can do so only with Germany's aid. 'Alliance with Germany will remain the only true means whereby England can make Asia and Africa serviceable for her future greatness, alliance with Germany not as she is today but with Germany

---

[3] *Ibid.*, pp. 341–2.

[4] Friedrich List, *Memorandum on the Value and the Conditions of an Alliance between Great Britain and Germany*, quoted by Franz Neumann in *Behemoth*, New York, 1943, p. 105.

as she ought to be and as she could become, with England's help.' England must recognize, List declares, that Germany cannot become strong on the basis of free trade. Free trade is a fit doctrine only for a nation that is already powerful. . . . Germany has to become so strong that she is able to keep England's competitors, France and Russia, at bay. . . . List was thus the first to develop the theory that Hitler brought to full flower in *Mein Kampf* and National Socialist foreign policy attempted to realize during the years preceding the German-Russian non-aggression pact of 1939: a redivision of the earth between Germany and England on the basis of German racial doctrines of superiority.[5]

Racial or social imperialism attempts to unify the nation by concessions to the masses, specifically the promise of full employment. An attempt is made to suppress internal class conflict through the demagogy of Social Darwinism applied to international relations (the 'white man's burden' or the 'mission of the Aryan race'). In England, the attempt to harness imperialism to social reform began in the 1890s. Hitler was but following an ideology previously articulated in England;[6] the characteristic features of this ideology being national unity, racial superiority, militant patriotism leading to aggressive wars, rationalized by the pseudo-science of geopolitics.

Social imperialism not only utilizes List's racial theory but also agrees with List's strictures on cosmopolitism:

A detailed criticism of tertiary economics was made in the House of Commons, January 30, 1908, by Austen Chamberlain, who had been Balfour's Chancellor from 1903–5. The British economy was faced with chronic unemployment, Chamberlain began. This was due not to intemperance, nor to the lack of education on the part of the workers, as some Radicals had claimed. The cause was more basic. Britons could be divided into those occupied in 'non-productive work and those who were engaged in the service of their fellows in one form or another'. The 1901 Census had indicated an increase, over the Census of 1881, of 19 per cent of those engaged in 'productive' work and of 41·2 per cent of those performing 'non-productive' work. . . . Un-

[5] Neumann, *op. cit.*, p. 105.
[6] Bernard Semmel, *Imperialism and Social Reform*, Cambridge, Massachusetts, 1960, p. 157. Semmel also shows that 'The Tariff Reformers were in many respects disciples of List. . . .' p. 155.

productive labour was the unskilled labour of carmen and dockers as well as much of the labour in commerce and service fields—in a word, unproductive work was work in the tertiary industries. . . . Unemployment, the Tariff Reformers were convinced, was largely due to the working out of a system of the 'cosmopolitan' capitalists and would be removed by the policy of the 'self-contained' empire.[7]

Social imperialism stresses the parasitic role of finance capitalism. The entrepreneur or industrialist capitalist furnishes employment and increases material output, thus building up the nation's strength; whereas, the banking interests, concerned only with profit, are prepared to sacrifice the national interest. In England, for example, during the tariff controversy, Sir Gilbert Parker, 'one of the more active speakers and writers for the Tariff Reform cause',[8] wrote as follows:

I don't believe that the interest upon a safe and sound investment in railway bonds or foreign loans, takes any place as an alternative against those natural profits which come from good investment in manufactures which give employment to the working man, which keep in the country, actively engaged, that energy, that paying energy, which is necessary for its progress and development.[9]

In England, as opposed to Germany and the United States, prior to World War I, there was no fusion of finance and industrial capital:

. . . everywhere except, significantly, in England, there has come into being a close alliance between high finance and the cartel magnates, often going as far as personal identity. Although the relation between capitalists and entrepreneurs is one of the typical and fundamental *conflicts* of the capitalist economy, monopoly capitalism has virtually fused the big banks and cartels into one.[10]

Semmel stresses this 'fundamental conflict' between the

[7] Semmel, *op. cit.*, pp. 157–8.
[8] Semmel, *op. cit.*, p. 157.
[9] Sir Gilbert Parker, *A National Policy: Our Fiscal and Imperial Reciprocity* (Gravesend, n.d.), p. 10. Quoted by Semmel, *op. cit.*, p. 157.
[10] Joseph A. Schumpeter, *Imperialism and Social Classes* (translated by Heinz Norden and edited by Paul M. Sweezy), New York, 1951, pp. 106–7.

entrepreneur and the capitalist to explain the failure of Joseph Chamberlain to achieve his tariff programme:

> The banks of England, luxuriating in the profits of England's position as the international clearing house, had no interest in going beyond the orthodox commercial banking policy of providing trade and other short-term credit. . . . In England, it was possible for the banker to contemplate the decline of British industry with equanimity.[11]

But Semmel also points out that there were other economic interests that supported free trade:

> British ship-builders . . . found their product still welcomed in protected continental markets, as well as, of course, in the home market. . . . Taking advantage of British Free Trade, German manufacturers 'dumped' steel at prices lower than German prices. The availability of cheap steel and ship-building skill helped to make it possible for Britain to reap full advantage of her position as an international entrepot and facilitated the development of a huge mercantile navy which served as a common carrier for the trade of all nations. Not only the ship-builders, but the new class of ship-owners which developed had an obvious stake in frustrating the design of the Tariff Reformers to turn inward and throw overboard the profits of the highly developed international common-carrier trade.
>
> Lancashire's cotton industry, too, ranged itself on the side of Free Trade. Not that Lancashire had not suffered from the competition of foreign textile mills sheltered behind protective tariff walls. . . . Yet despite the closing down of continental and American markets for British cotton piece-goods, Lancashire's cotton exports continued to grow. . . . Lancashire required cheap food and cheap raw materials which it believed tariffs would endanger. . . . The 'organized' working class—remembering the stories of the hungry 'forties and cherishing the cheap loaf—remained loyal to Free Trade. . . . The industries committed to Free Trade . . . contained the bulk of the working class: in the textile industries were 1,500,000 workers; there were 1,000,000 coal miners (British coal exports were most welcome even in protected marketing areas); 200,000 seamen; 1,000,000 engaged in ship-building; 1,250,000 in various transportation enterprises.[12]

[11] Semmel, *op. cit.*, p. 145.
[12] *Ibid.*, pp. 146–8.

Anti-Classical Theories in the Twentieth Century

In Germany,

National Socialist anti-capitalism has always exempted productive capital, that is, industrial capital, from its denunciations and solely concentrated on 'predatory' (that is, banking) capital. But even the fight against banking capital was only a sham. On 14 October 1930, the National Socialist parliamentary group introduced into the democratic parliament a draft bill demanding the confiscation without indemnity of the 'entire property of the bank and stock exchange barons, of the eastern Jews, and of other foreigners who had entered after 1 August 1914, and of all additional property acquired through war, revolution, inflation, or deflation after that date'. When the Communists and Social Democrats declared their intention of voting for the bill, the National Socialists quickly withdrew their motion. Still the attack against 'predatory' as opposed to 'productive' capital did not cease; on the contrary, it increased by leaps and bounds. The slogan was no doubt popular—a bank is always a creditor of the small and little businessman and, therefore, hated as a creditor usually is. Interests on loans are no doubt not the outcome of productive labour, though they are necessary within the capitalistic system. Finance capital as identified with banking capital has always been the target of all pseudo-socialist movements, movements that never dared to touch the foundations of capitalist society but rather sought a reform that would break the poisonous teeth off the capitalist system and direct the deep resentment of the masses against exploitation toward concrete symbols. Whether the chosen symbol is John Pierpont Morgan or a Jewish banker is immaterial.

In singling out predatory capital, National Socialism treads in the footsteps of Proudhon, who, in his *Idée Générale de la Révolution au 19ᵉ Siècle*, demanded the liquidation of the Banque de France and its transformation into an institution of 'public utility' together with a lowering of interest to one-half or one-fourth of 1 per cent. The *Communist Manifesto* had already denounced that type of Socialism, the so-called 'True Socialism', as specifically Germanic. Marx, in a letter to Engels on 8 August 1851, had, with supreme wit, denounced Proudhon's fight against banking capital and interest as a sham. He had already pointed out that the so-called 'social liquidation' is 'merely the means of starting afresh the healthy bourgeois society'.[13]

[13] Franz Neumann, *Behemoth*, New York, 1942, pp. 320–1.

120

Neumann gives the following summary of the relation between industrial and banking capital:[14]

... in the early stage of large-scale industry, capital formation within industry is not sufficient for expansion. Industry needs large amounts of capital in single lumps. The banks organize the credit system by canalizing the savings of the masses, especially to the railroads. In this period the demand for money capital is indeed high, and correspondingly the power of the banks, whether in the form of the private investment banker as in the United States, or in that of the joint stock banks as in Germany. In the second phase, however, the accumulation of capital within industry increases to such an extent that industry becomes almost independent of the banks and is able to finance expansion out of undistributed profits. In the final phase, that of National Socialist monopoly economy, industry is often incapable of investing all its savings in its plant. It begins to expand into almost any other economic activity, and even begins to conquer banks and insurance institutions—and thereby assumes the role of the finance capitalist.[15]

In Germany and England (as well as in the United States and France) there was a transient historical conflict, but not a 'fundamental' one, between industrial and banking capital.[16] Nevertheless, Nazi ideology emphasized this so-called basic conflict, and, of course, the Jews were the scapegoats. The Jews were a people apart, hence cosmopolitan; Marx was Jewish and had called upon the workers of the world to establish an international organization; Jews were bankers, etc.

The Marxian economic distinction between productive and unproductive labour, where banking is an expense of circulation and hence unproductive of surplus value, is transmuted by the ideology of social imperialism into a spurious conflict

---

[14] Neumann follows Henryk Grossman's schema. Grossman was criticizing Rudolph Hilferding's theory of the dominance of finance capital (*Das Finanzkapital*, Vienna, 1910). Grossman showed that at the time Hilferding wrote industry had already become independent of the banks. *Das Akkumulations-und Zusammenbruchesgesetz des kapitalistichen Systems*, Leipzig, 1929, pp. 572–9.

[15] Neumann, *op. cit.*, p. 322.

[16] 'The alleged conflict of industry and finance, once real, is now true only of that section of industry, still large but not dominant, that minds its own business. But though these capitalists are still important, they do not set the "tone" of industrial upswing and crash.' William J. Blake, *op. cit.* p. 384.

between 'predatory' and 'productive' capital. Its reactionary character has been well stated by Neumann:

> Whenever the outcry against the sovereignty of banking capital is injected into a popular movement, it is the surest sign that fascism is on its way.[17]

The Nazi attack on cosmopolitanism and 'predatory' capital provided the rationale of 'people's imperialism':

> Racial proletarianism is the genuine theory of National Socialism. . . . National Socialism offers the worker everything offered by Marxism, and without a class struggle. National Socialism offers him a higher form of life, 'the people's community', and the rule of labour over money, without compelling him to fight against his own ruling class. On the contrary, he is invited to join the ruling classes, to share in their power, glory, and material benefits by being a part of a colossal machine. . . . Germany's victory is his victory, the victory of labour over money, of the people's community over class rule, of true freedom over a liberty that was merely a cloak for exploitation.[18]

Ricardo's new chapter 'On Machinery' opened a 'Pandora's Box' on conflict:[19] because (1) substitution of capital for labour might increase net revenue at the expense of gross revenue and (2) independently of the effects of machinery, the workers have a direct interest in how the net revenue is expended since, as John Stuart Mill later puts it, 'demand for commodities is not demand for labour'.[20] The Ricardian conflict between capitalists and workers, i.e. the conflict between accumulation (productive expenditures) and employment (unproductive expenditures) is transmuted by Nazi Neomercantilists into a conflict between industrial and banking or international capital, where the latter is held to be parasitic.

In summary, the Ricardian conflict between capital and labour is transformed into pseudo-conflict between productive and parasitic capital. As has been indicated, this supposedly basic conflict was articulated long after the merger of industrial and banking (finance) capital. Because Nazi ideology accepted

---

[17] Neumann, *op. cit.*, p. 322.
[18] *Ibid.*, pp. 189–90.
[19] *Supra*, Chap. III.
[20] John Stuart Mill, *Principles of Political Economy* (Ashley edition) seventh edition, 1871, pp. 79 ff.

the existing social relations of production and further because Nazi demagogy required a radical façade, it was essential to stress the conflict between production and circulation (even after their integration) rather than the conflict between labour and capital.

(B) KEYNESIAN ANTI-CLASSICAL SOLUTION

When my new theory has been duly assimilated and mixed with politics and feelings and passions, I can't predict what the final upshot will be in its effect on action and affairs. But there will be a great change, and, in particular, the Ricardian foundations of Marxism will be knocked away. J. M. Keynes to George Bernard Shaw, 1st January 1935, quoted by R. F. Harrod in *The Life of John Maynard Keynes*, New York, 1951, p. 462.

A consequence of the 'marginalist revolution' in the last quarter of the nineteenth century was the abandonment of the distinction between productive and unproductive labour. The substitution of a utility-scarcity for the labour theory of value—the generalization of the Ricardian theory of rent to all factors of production, with the stress on the co-ordinate contribution of each of these factors—precluded a distinction between productive and unproductive labour.[21]

Keynes accepted Neoclassical value theory although rejecting Say's Law of Markets. However, both Keynesian and post-Keynesian economic thought contain either explicitly or implicitly a distinction between productive and unproductive consumption. Whereas for Classical economists productive consumption was consumption by labour-power that yielded a surplus, Keynesian analysis considers any consumption in

[21] Nassau W. Senior anticipated the Neoclassical rejection of Adam Smith's distinction between productive and unproductive labour: 'I cannot . . . account for his stating that capital is dedicated to the maintenance of productive labourers and revenue to that of the unproductive . . . the difference between saving and spending is to be found in distinguishing not productive from unproductive labour or commodities from services, but . . . productive from unproductive consumption.' *Industrial Efficiency and Social Economy* (edited by S. Leon Levy), New York, 1923, Vol. I, pp. 141–2. But, as Leo Rogin pointed out, 'does not Senior himself denote as all-important "abstinence", the action of a person who "abstains from the unproductive use of what he can command"? And is not the use of revenue in the employment of domestic servants an "unproductive use" in this connection?' *The Meaning and Validity of Economic Theory*, New York, 1956, p. 264.

excess of the supply-price of a factor of production as unproductive, viz.

> Thus we may define 'unproductive consumption' as consumption which could be foregone by the consumer without reacting on the amount of his productive effort, and 'productive consumption' as consumption which could not be foregone without such a reaction. . . . So long as unemployment and unproductive consumption are allowed to exist side by side, present total net income and future available income are less than they might be; and nothing is required to mend the situation except a method of transferring consumption from one set of individuals to another.[22]

Keynes' transfer mechanism is a profit (not an income) inflation, i.e. a fall in real wages:

> . . the evil of not creating wealth would be greater than the evil that the wealth, when created, should not accrue to those who have made the sacrifice, namely, to the consumers whose consumption has been curtailed by the higher prices consequent on the Profit Inflation.[23]

The distinction between productive and unproductive consumption is implicit in Keynes' *General Theory*. Here Keynes argued that workers stipulate for a money and not a real wage, from which Keynes concluded that a rise in prices unaccompanied by an increase in money wages does not reduce the supply of labour. According to this analysis, the market price of labour-power lies above its supply price. The excess of the market price over the supply price constitutes unproductive consumption.[24]

In the 'Concluding Notes' of the *General Theory*, Keynes

[22] J. M. Keynes, *A Treatise on Money*, New York, 1930, Vol. II, pp. 125–7.
[23] *Ibid.*, p. 126. In a subsequent passage Keynes expresses a 'preference for a policy today which, whilst avoiding Deflation at all costs, aims at the stability of purchasing power as its ideal objective. Perhaps the ultimate solution lies in the rate of capital development becoming more largely an affair of state, determined by collective wisdom and long views'. p. 163.
[24] *The General Theory of Employment Interest and Money*, New York, 1936, pp. 17 ff. Keynesian short-run analysis assumed the 'law' of diminishing returns, hence real wages must fall *pari passu* with the decline in labour's marginal product. But if real wages must decline then obviously there must have been unproductive consumption, otherwise there would be the complicating difficulty of obtaining an adequate supply of labour.

departs from his static model to offer some observations on the future. Here, too, the distinction between productive and unproductive consumption appears. Now, however, it is the capitalist *qua* rentier whose consumption is unproductive:

> ... The scale of investment is promoted by a *low* rate of interest. ... Thus it is to our best advantage to reduce the rate of interest to that point relatively [sic] to the schedule of the marginal efficiency of capital at which there is full employment ... yet it would mean the euthanasia of the rentier, and, consequently, the euthanasia of the cumulative oppressive power of the capitalist to exploit the scarcity-value of capital. Interest today rewards no genuine sacrifice, any more than does the rent of land.[25]

In Keynesian analysis, then, as in right-wing Neomercantilist thought, a presumed conflict exists between industrial and banking capital.

(C) POST KEYNESIAN DYNAMIC ANALYSIS

Post-Keynesian dynamic economics has its origin in an article by Keynes on the economic effects of a declining population.[26] Keynes argued that the demand for capital depends on (1) the standard of living, (2) the period of production and (3) population growth:

> Let us consider the period of just over fifty years from 1860 to 1913. I find no evidence of any important change in the length of the technical period of production. Statistics ... we have do not suggest that there have been large changes in the amount of capital employed to produce a unit of output ... the increased demand was primarily attributable to the increasing population and to the rising standard of life, and only in a minor degree to technical changes of a kind which called for an increasing capitalization per unit of consumption. . . . The population figures, which are reliable, indicate that about half the increase in capital was required to serve the increasing population. Perhaps the figures were about as follows, though I would emphasize that these conclusions are very rough and to be regarded only as broad pointers to what was going on:

[25] *Ibid.*, pp. 375–6.
[26] 'Some Economic Consequences of a Declining Population', *Eugenics Review*, April 1937.

	1860	1913
Real Capital	100	270
Population	100	150
Standard of life	100	160
Period of Production	100	110

It follows that a stationary population with the same improvement in the standard of life and the same lengthening of the period of production would have required an increase in the stock of capital of only a little more than half of the increase which actually occurred.[27]

Keynes next develops a growth model: On the assumption that saving under 'full employment lies somewhere between 8 and 15 per cent' of national income and that the capital-output ratio is about 4:1, then the stock of capital must grow 'between 2 and 4 per cent per annum'.[28] Algebraically, Ig is the rate of growth of investment, S is the percentage saved of national income, and C is the capital-output ratio. Hence, $Ig = S/C$. But since the capital-output ratio is fixed, it follows that income (Y) must grow at the same rate as investment.

Keynes classifies investments into two types, viz. investments that 'enable a unit of capital to yield a unit of product with the aid of less labour than before, and those which lead to a change in the amount of capital employed *more* than in proportion to the resulting output'. The first type of investments will continue, Keynes believes, and will absorb about half of the proportion of income saved at full employment. However, Keynes is pessimistic about improvements that would raise the capital-output ratio. His policy recommendations are two: (1) a lowering of the rate of interest, which would tend to lengthen the period of production, and (2) a redistribution of income that would lower the proportion saved.[29]

Subsequently, Harrod developed a growth model along the lines suggested by Keynes.[30] But first, Harrod contrasts his model with the dynamic model of classical economics:

[27] *Ibid.*, pp. 14–15.
[28] *Ibid.*, p. 15.
[29] *Ibid.*, p. 16.
[30] R. F. Harrod, 'An Essay in Dynamic Theory', *The Economic Journal*, March 1939. Subsequently, Harrod extended his analysis in *Towards a Dynamic Economics*, London, 1956.

In the old economics accumulation was the motive power. Here we have a stark contradiction to Keynesian doctrine in which saving is always tending to retard advance. . . . there are two propositions in the classical system which can be tentatively discarded. . . . we may regard the size of population not, as in the old classical system, as a dependent but as an independent variable. To put the matter otherwise, changes in it may be regarded as exogenous. Secondly, I propose to discard the law of diminishing returns from the land as a primary determinant in a progressive economy.[31]

In developing his growth model, Harrod proceeds with the truism that $GC = s$ (or s-k where k is autonomous investment); G is growth of output, C is the capital-output ratio, and s is the fraction of income saved. Harrod finds this equation highly significant: 'I know of no alternative formulation, in the world of modern economic theory, of any dynamic principle of comparable generality.[32] (Since the capital-output ratio is constant, Harrod's geometric growth rate for output is the same as the Keynesian growth rate for investment.)

Harrod next defines a warranted growth rate, i.e. that rate of growth 'which, if executed will leave entrepreneurs in a state of mind in which they are prepared to carry on a similar advance'.[33] The equation is as follows: $G_w C_r = s$; where G_w is the warranted rate of growth, C_r is the amount of new capital required divided by the increment of output (as a simplifying assumption, Harrod makes the average and marginal values equal) and s is the percentage saved out of income. Harrod's warranted growth rate is consistent with unemployment. It is a rate that satisfies entrepreneurs but not necessarily workers.

Thus, there is an actual rate of growth, $GC = s$, and a warranted rate of growth, $G_w C_r = s$:

Taking these two equations together, we can see a relation of utmost simplicity, and I ask you to join with me in thinking it extraordinarily impressive. The greater G, the lower C. That can hardly be questioned. Consequently if G has a value above G_w, C will have a value below C_r. I see no escape from that. If C has a value below C_r, this means that on balance producers and traders find the goods in the pipe-line or the equipment insuf-

[31] *Towards a Dynamic Economics*, pp. 19–20.
[32] *Ibid.*, p. 80.
[33] *Ibid.*, p. 82.

ficient to sustain existing turnover. . . . if the actual growth is above the line of growth consistent with a steady advance, orders will be increased. And, of course, conversely. This strikes me as an extraordinarily simple and notable demonstration of the instability of an advancing system. . . . G is a quantity determined from time to time by trial and error, by the collective trials and errors of vast numbers of people. It would be great luck if their collective appraisals caused them to hit precisely upon the value of G_w. But if they do not do so their experience will tend to drive them farther and farther from it.[34]

Besides an actual and a warranted rate of growth, Harrod has a natural rate of growth, i.e. a rate of growth determined by population increase and technological progress, which are considered exogenous. The natural growth rate is a long-run maximum feasible rate. This rate sets a physical limit to the actual and warranted growth rates:

Whenever G exceeds G_w there will be a tendency for a boom to develop; and conversely. Now if G_n exceeds G_w there is no reason why the economy should not enjoy a recurrent tendency to develop boom conditions. But if G_w exceeds G_n, then G must lie below G_w for most of the time, since the average value of G over a period cannot exceed that of G_n. . . . Saving *is* a virtue and beneficial so long as G_w is below G_n. . . . by raising G_w, it enables us to have good employment without inflation. But if G_w is above G_n saving is a force making for depression.[35]

Here, then, is the clue to the trade cycle. The actual rate of growth may be above or below the warranted. But, Harrod implies, there is no probability of a bias in either direction. However, if the warranted rate lies above the natural, the tendency is towards chronic depression. For Harrod, the recovery process results in a depression because the warranted growth rate exceeds the natural growth rate:

If G_w is very substantially above G_n, G may never rise very far above G_w during the revival owing to mobility difficulties, and in this case maintenance of the revival may be precarious, and a vicious spiral of depression may be precipitated long before full employment is reached.[36]

[34] *Ibid.*, pp. 85–6.
[35] *Ibid.*, pp. 88–9.
[36] *Ibid.*, p. 90.

It is important to emphasize that the natural rate of growth, to which Harrod attaches strategic importance, is exogenously determined. Essentially, in Harrod's model, the excess of the warranted rate over the natural arises from a population shortage. Also, it must be pointed out, Harrod provides no empirical data to substantiate his hypothesis. Nor is this to be wondered about inasmuch as the data available contradict his thesis:

> If prosperity comes to an end because national income *cannot* grow sufficiently fast to prevent an excessive accumulation of capital, we should observe a severe shortage of labour and rapidly rising prices, a phenomenon apparently absent in 1907, 1929, and 1937.[37]

Such is Domar's conclusion. Domar also developed a model of economic growth, which stresses the capacity effect on investment as well as the income generating effect.[38] Domar's contribution has been recognized by contemporary followers of Keynes, e.g. reference is usually made to the Harrod-Domar growth model.[39] Incidentally, Domar refuses to commit himself to an explanation of the cause of depressions.

Neither in Keynes' dynamic model, nor in the Harrod-Domar growth model is there any reference to the distinction between productive and unproductive labour. However, Kaldor's exposition of the Keynesian long-run theory of distribution, coupled with his use of the Harrod growth model, requires the existence of unproductive consumption by the working class—'unproductive' in the Keynesian sense that a decrease in workers' consumption has no adverse effect on the supply of labour.

The thesis that in the contemporary period the market price of labour-power is above its cost of production is based on the view that industrial capitalism can be divided into two stages, viz: a primary phase of accumulation in which wages

[37] Evsey D. Domar, *Essays in the Theory of Economic Growth*, New York, 1957, p. 117.

[38] 'Expansion and Employment', *The American Economic Review*, March 1947, reprinted in *op. cit.*

[39] In Marxian terminology, the Harrod-Domar model reveals a conflict between 'the forces of production' (supply) and 'the relations of productions' (demand). However, modern Keynesian growth theorists believe it possible to resolve this conflict by social engineering within a capitalist framework.

are at a subsistence minimum; and a subsequent stage during which real wages exceed the cost of production of labour-power.[40]

For the first phase of industrialization, it is recognized that the Ricardo-Marxian model is a useful analytical tool. In the Ricardo-Marxian model, profits (surplus-value) are a residual, i.e. profits (P) are equal to income (Y) minus wage payments (variable capital). However, this stage is superseded by one where the real wage exceeds the cost of labour-power. In this second stage, assuming that workers consume all of their income, profits are equal to the sum of investment and capitalist consumption:

> ... here wages (not profits) are a residue, profits being governed by the propensity to invest and the capitalists' propensity to consume, which represent a kind of 'prior charge' on the national output. Whereas in the Ricardian model the ultimate incidence of all taxes (other than taxes on rent) falls on profits, here the incidence of all taxes, taxes on income and profits as well as on commodities, falls on wages.[41]

The thesis that the market price of labour-power lies above its cost of production was implicit in Keynes' 'widow's cruse' analogy:

> If entrepreneurs choose to spend a portion of their profits on consumption (and there is, of course, nothing to prevent them from doing this) the effect is to increase the profits on the sale of liquid consumption goods by an amount exactly equal to the amount of profits which have been thus expended. . . . Thus,

[40] An explicit formulation of the two-stage thesis of capitalism was first developed by Nicholas Kaldor in 'Alternative Theories of Distribution'- *Review of Economic Studies*, Vol. XXIII, No. 2, 1955–6, reprinted in Kaldor's *Essays on Value and Distribution*, London, 1960, pp. 209 ff. Subsequently, Kaldor re-iterated the thesis in 'Capitalist Evolution in the Light of Keynesian Economics', a lecture given at the University of Peking, May 11, 1956, and also in 'A Model of Economic Growth', *Economic Journal*, December 1957. The last two essays are reprinted in Kaldor's *Essays on Economic Growth and Stability*, London, 1960. However, the two stages theory of capitalist development is implicit in Michael Kalecki's analysis. According to Kalecki, monopoly power in modern capitalist society is such as to ensure a fixed mark-up by capitalists over prime costs (cost of materials and wages) so that the ratio of aggregate proceeds of industry to aggregate prime costs of industry is constant. Such being the case, 'profits are determined by capitalists' consumption and investment'. M. Kalecki, *Theory of Economic Dynamics*, London, 1954, p. 47.

[41] 'Alternative Theories of Distribution', *op. cit.*, pp. 230–1.

however much of their profits entrepreneurs spend on consumption, the increment of wealth belonging to entrepreneurs remains the same as before. Thus profits, as a source of capital increment for entrepreneurs, are a widow's cruse which remains undepleted however much of them may be devoted to riotous living. When on the other hand, entrepreneurs are making losses, and seek to recoup these losses by curtailing their normal expenditure on consumption, i.e. by saving more, the cruse becomes a Danaid jar which can never be filled up; for the effect of this reduced expenditure is to inflict on the producers of consumption-goods a loss of an equal amount. Thus the diminution of their wealth as a class is as great, in spite of their savings, as it was before.[42]

Thus, as Kaldor has emphasized, the Keynesian analysis can be applied to either employment or distribution problems:

The reason why the multiplier-analysis has not been developed as a distribution theory is precisely because it was invented for the purpose of an employment theory—to explain why an economic system can remain in equilibrium in a state of under-employment (or a general under-utilization of resources), where the classical properties of scarcity-economics are inapplicable. And its use for the one appears to exclude its use for the other. If we assume that the balance of savings and investment is brought about through variations in the relationship of prices and costs, we are not only bereft of a principle for explaining variations in output and employment, but the whole idea of separate 'aggregate' demand and supply functions—the principle of 'effective demand'—falls to the ground; we are back to Say's Law, where output as a whole is limited by available resources, and a fall in effective demand for one commodity (in real terms) generates compensating increases in effective demand (again in real terms) for others. Yet these two uses of the Multiplier principle are not as incompatible as would appear at first sight: the Keynesian technique . . . can be used for both

[42] J. M. Keynes, *Treatise on Money*, Vol. I, p. 139. According to Kaldor, 'This passage, I think, contains the true seed of the ideas developed in the *General Theory*. . . . The fact that "profits", "savings", etc., were all defined here in a special sense that was later discarded, and that the argument specifically refers to expenditure on consumption goods, rather than entrepreneurial expenditure in general, should not blind us to the fact that here Keynes regards entrepreneurial incomes as being the resultant of their expenditure decisions, rather than the other way around—which is perhaps the most important difference between "Keynesian" and "pre-Keynesian" habits of thought.' Nicholas Kaldor, 'Alternative Theories of Distribution', *op. cit.*, p. 227, n. 1.

purposes, provided the one is conceived as a short-run theory and the other as a long-run theory—or rather, the one is used in the framework of a static model, and the other in the framework of a dynamic growth model.[43]

Kaldor's exposition of the dynamic model is as follows: (1) assume only two classes in society, then income is equal to wages plus profits ($Y = W + P$); and (2) assume also that workers consume all of their income, then the profit formula is $P = \dfrac{1}{s} I$, where s is the percentage of profits saved by entrepreneurs, and I equals investment.[44] The share of profits in the income then becomes $\dfrac{P}{Y} = K \dfrac{I}{Y}$, where k is the multiplier, i.e. the reciprocal of the entrepreneurs' propensity to save from profits. In short, the income multiplier is the profit multiplier:

> The critical assumption is that the investment/output ratio is an independent variable. . . . we can describe the determinants of the investment/output ratio in terms of the rate of growth of output capacity (G) and the capital/output ratio, v:
>
> $$\frac{I}{Y} = Gv$$
>
> In a state of continuous full employment G must be equal to the rate of growth of the 'full employment ceiling', i.e. the sum of the rate of technical progress and the growth in working population. . . . The model . . . shows the share of profits P/Y, the rate of profit on capital P/vY, and the real wage rate W/L, as functions of I/Y which in turn is determined independently of P/Y or W/L.[45]

But, as Kaldor points out, there are four reasons that the investment-output ratio may not be an independent variable: First, the real wage must be equal to or greater than the cost of production ('subsistence minimum') of labour-power. In

[43] *Ibid.*, pp. 227–8.
[44] Actually, Kaldor's model does include workers' savings. Kaldor's constraint is that the marginal propensity to save of entrepreneurs from profits exceeds that of the workers from wages. However, Kaldor does consider the limiting case where workers' savings are zero. For expository reasons, we have concentrated on this model.
[45] *Ibid.*, pp. 231–2.

the event that the real wage is below the cost of production of labour-power, the profit-income ratio (P/Y) will be dependent upon the real wage (W/L) since the increased demand for labour consequent upon a rise in the growth rate will increase real wages and hence depress the profit-income ratio. Conversely, if real wages were below the cost of production of labour-power *and did not rise* with the increased demand for labour because of (say) some institutional obstacle, dynamic equilibrium could not be maintained because of the consequent population shortage.

Second, 'the indicated share of profits cannot be below the level which yields the minimum rate of profit necessary to induce the capitalists to invest their capital and which we may call the risk "premium rate".' Third, if because of market imperfections, there exists a monopoly of profit, then the share of profits in income must be such as to equal or exceed this monopoly rate. The second and third constraints 'describe *alternative* restrictions, of which the higher will apply'. The fourth constraint requires that the capital-output ratio, v, must be independent of the profit share, P/Y; otherwise, given the rate of growth, G, I/Y will be dependent upon the rate of profit, P/vY:

A certain degree of dependence follows inevitably from the consideration . . . that the value of particular capital goods will vary with the rate of profit, so that, even with a *given technique*, v will not be independent of P/Y. (We shall ignore this point.) There is the further complication that the relation P/Y may affect v through making more or less 'labour-saving' techniques profitable. In other words, at any given wage-price relationship, the producers will adopt the technique which maximizes the rate of profit on capital, P/vY; this will affect (at a given G) I/Y, and hence P/Y. Hence any rise in P/Y will reduce v, and thus I/Y, and conversely, any rise in I/Y will raise P/Y. If the sensitiveness of v to P/Y is great, P/Y can no longer be regarded as being determined by the equations of the model; the *technical* relation between v and P/Y will then govern P/Y whereas the savings equation . . . will determine I/Y and thus (given G) the value of v.[46]

Subject to the above constraints, and given the assumption

[46] *Ibid.*, pp. 233–4.

of full employment, Kaldor concludes that the Keynesian multiplier principle provides a long-run theory of distribution. According to Kaldor, Keynes' and Kalecki's theory of distribution can be paraphrased as 'capitalists earn what they spend, and workers spend what they earn'.[47]

The assumption that real wages exceed the supply price of labour-power apparently is justified on the grounds that since about the mid-nineteenth century there has been a secular rise in real wages in industrialized countries. But a rise in the selling price of a commodity does not constitute *prima facie* evidence that its market price is above its supply price. Rather, before one could establish such a proposition, it would be necessary to determine what changes, if any, had taken place in the cost of production of the commodity.

Historic changes in the cost of production of labour-power can be summarized as follows: From about the fifteenth century to beyond the middle of the nineteenth century there was a secular fall in the value of labour-power, viz. handicraft production with its apprenticeship system was superseded by the domestic system in which division and subdivision of labour reduced the average cost of labour-power, i.e. there occurred a reduction in the skills and preliminary training requisite for carrying on production. The importance of child labour in the Mercantilist period was well appreciated by Petty, who included children seven years or older among his productive labourers. Subsequently, the substitution of the labour of women and children for that of the adult male during the industrial revolution of the eighteenth and nineteenth centuries continued this secular tendency.[48] The history of the trade union movement confirms the analysis:

> The origin of trade unions can, in many cases, be definitely traced to the encroachments of the merchant-capitalist upon the standard of life of the mechanics. . . . the workmen demanded a minimum wage below which none was to work irrespective of the quality of the product. . . . To further safeguard their standard of life they also demanded a strict observance of apprenticeship rules, which would automatically eliminate the

---

[47] *Ibid.*, p. 230.
[48] See my *Population Theories and the Economic Interpretation* (London and New York), 1957, Ch. VIII, 'Demand for Labour'.

competition of woman, child, unskilled, and convict labour. ... the early unions were composed exclusively of skilled workers like printers, shoemakers, tailors, carpenters, and so on. ... On the other hand no traces of organization can be found among the unskilled, especially the cotton-mill operatives who numbered 100,000 in 1815. This is explained by the fact that the wages [rather family income] of the unskilled were going up while those of the skilled were kept down. ... This contrast in their conditions appears in the shoe industry. The shoemakers of Lynn, Massachusetts, manufactured, on the whole, the cheaper grades of shoes. This made it possible to subdivide the work so that the entire family could be employed. Hence while the income of the head of the family, under the merchant-capitalist system, was not as large as formerly, the total income of the family actually increased.[49]

Now this four to five century depreciation of the value (cost) of labour-power was reversed in the latter part of the nineteenth century. Modern technology requires a literate, well-trained labour force, whose symptoms are mechanics institutes, the Education Acts, and today the increased percentage of students enrolled in colleges. Again, the shift from primary into secondary and tertiary industries, with the concomitant occupational changes, raises the average cost of labour-power.[50] It is apparent, then, that merely to regard changes in real wages, without considering historic changes in the cost of labour-power, is to adopt a superficial approach.

Incidentally, the theory that the strategic variable for population growth is the ratio of income to cost of labour-power illuminates the observed long-run stability or upward shift in the consumption function.[51]

Kaldor's assumption that I/Y is the independent variable in the profit equation, $\frac{P}{Y} = \frac{I}{sY}$, can be better appreciated following a disaggregation of the Keynesian system along the lines suggested by Marx. Similarly, an evaluation of Kaldor's explanation of cyclical phenomena also must be postponed.

---

[49] John R. Commons and Associates, *History of Labor in the United States*, New York (sixth printing), 1951, Vol. I, pp. 104–5.

[50] See my *op. cit.*, pp. 176 ff.

[51] See the Appendix to this chapter, 'Classical Economics and the Deusenberry Hypothesis'.

Anti-Classical Theories in the Twentieth Century

A Disaggregated Model of the Keynesian System:

Assumptions:
1. Only two classes in society, hence income (Y) equals profits (P) and wages (W).
2. Workers consume all of their income.
3. Profits are divided between investment and consumption expenditures. Decisions to save are decisions to invest, i.e. Say's Law of Markets holds.
4. Sector I produces capital goods for itself and for the consumer sector (2), e.g. $I_{1s} + I_{2s} = I_s$, supply of investment goods.
5. Sector 2 produces consumer goods for itself and for the investment sector (1), e.g. $C_{1s} + C_{2s} = C_s$, the supply of consumer goods.

Definitions:
1. $Y = C + I (\equiv S) \equiv P + W$
2. $P + W \equiv P_1 + P_2 + W_1 + W_2$
3. $I_s = P_1 + W_1$ and $C_s = P_2 + W_2$ (subscript s is supply)
4. $I_d = aP_1 + \alpha P_2$ (where subscript d is demand, and a and α are average propensities to save [invest] of entrepreneurs in the investment and consumer goods sectors, respectively)
5. $C_d = W_1 + W_2 + bP_1 + \beta P_2$ (where subscript d is demand, and b and β are average propensities to consume of entrepreneurs in the investment and consumer goods sectors, respectively.)
6. $a + b = 1$ and $\alpha + \beta = 1$

Equilibrium Condition—Supply equals demand:

$I_s = I_d$

$P_1 + W_1 = aP_1 + \alpha P_2$ (from definitions 3 and 4)

$aP_1 + bP_1 + W_1 = aP_1 + \alpha P_2$ (from definition 6)

$bP_1 + W_1 = \alpha P_2$ cancelling identical terms gives the equilibrium condition.

Similarly:

$C_s = C_d$

$P_2 + W_2 = W_1 + W_2 + bP_1 + \beta P_2$ (from definitions 3 and 5)

$\alpha P_2 + \beta P_2 + W_2 = W_1 + W_2 + bP_1 + \beta P_2$ (from definition 6)

$\alpha P_2 = bP_1 + W_1$ cancelling identical terms gives the equilibrium condition.

It may be helpful to think of the two sector model in terms

136

of international trade, viz. island A makes nothing but investment goods, part of which it sells to island B; whereas, island B produces nothing but consumer goods, part of which it exchanges with A for investment goods in order to produce its consumer goods. The equilibrium condition states that island A must purchase consumer goods from B equal in value to the investment goods A sells to B and *vice versa*.

The model emphasizes the interdependence of investment and consumption expenditures. Increased expenditures on capital goods in sector 2, the consumer sector, require increased entrepreneurial outlays for consumer goods and/or increased wage payments by the entrepreneurs of sector 1, the investment sector. Such is the equilibrium condition for balanced growth. *En passant*, abstractly considered, the model is compatible with rising unemployment, i.e. Marx's industrial reserve army.

How does the model compare with Kaldor's? For Kaldor, I/Y is the independent variable in the profit equation, $\frac{P}{Y} = \frac{I}{sY}$, and $I/Y = Gv$, where v is technologically given and invariant to P/Y. Thus, the more rapid the rate of growth of the economy, the greater the I/Y ratio and the greater the profit share. Translating Kaldor's I/Y into our terminology we obtain:

$$I/Y = \frac{aP_1 + aP_2}{Y}$$

but $aP_2 = bP_1 + W_1$ so

$$I/Y = \frac{aP_1 + bP_1 + W_1}{Y}$$

It is of course a tautology that I/Y is the ratio of entrepreneurs' and workers' income in sector 1 to total net income. However, recognition of the equilibrium condition for balanced growth elucidates a constraint not explicit in Kaldor's model. The equilibrium condition states I/Y is in part determined by the consumption expenditures of entrepreneurs and workers in sector 1. In Kaldor's model I/Y is determined by Gv and since v is invariant, G, the rate of growth, is crucial. According to Kaldor, G is determined by entrepreneurial optimism, and provided only that entrepreneurial optimism does not outrun the material base of economic progress, presumably all would be well. Whereas Harrod finds the cause of cyclical difficulty arising from excessive saving, Kaldor states:

> . . . the causes of cyclical movements should be sought in the disharmony between entrepreneurs' *desired* growth rate (as influenced by the degree of optimism and the volatility of expectations) which governs the rate of increase of output capacity (G), and the natural growth rate (dependent on technical progress and the growth of the working population) which governs the rate of growth of output over longer periods (let us call this G'). It is the excess of G over G'—not the excess of s over $G'v$—which causes periodic breakdowns in the investment process through the growth in output capacity outrunning the growth in production.[52]

The thesis that the excess G over G' precipitates a depression is unsupported by any data. Incidentally, according to Kaldor, this was essentially Marx's view: Marx believed that

> . . . in time as accumulation proceeds faster and faster, the demand for wage-labour must also increase faster and faster, hence it must sooner or later overtake the increase in supply, and thereby extinguish the 'reserve army'. When this happens, wages rise and profits fall since the factor which previously tied wages to the subsistence level—the excess of job-seekers over the number of jobs available—is no longer present.[53]

Kaldor here confuses historical periods. It is true that in the period of primitive accumulation—Mercantilism—the shortage of population is typical and resolved by 'the turning of Africa into a warren for the commercial hunting of black skins'.[54] However, in the period of industrial capital accumulation, the substitution of capital for labour resolves the labour shortage. In other words, accumulation now operates to eliminate a labour shortage.

Kaldor argues that the excess of G over G' precipitates a depression rather than a smooth transition from a higher to a

---

[52] 'Alternative Theories of Distribution', *op. cit.*, p. 232. Kaldor holds that although in the short-run G exceeds G', in the long-run G' tends to adjust itself to G since when G is large 'the rapid growth in the supply of consumer goods also stimulates the growth in population'. 'Capitalist Evolution and Keynesian Economics', *op. cit.*, pp. 254–5.

[53] 'Capitalist Evolution in the Light of Keynesian Economics', *op. cit.*, pp. 248–9.

[54] *Capital*, Vol. I, p. 823. See also my *op. cit.*, pp. 110 ff.

lower growth rate. Short-run maladjustments are due to institutional and/or frictional obstacles. Thus a fall in G should reduce I/Y and hence P/Y. The reduction in the share of profits in national income is essential for obtaining the compensatory increase in consumption (a rise in labour's share in national income) that will maintain aggregate demand. If, however, monopoly prevents the decline in the P/Y, the equilibrating mechanism fails to operate. Again, even in the absence of monopoly, the fact that 'investment goods and consumption goods are produced by different industries, with limited mobility between them' means that profit margins may not fall sufficiently in the consumer sector. Again, on the upswing, the desired rate of growth of entrepreneurs may be frustrated by the downward inflexibility of real wages, thus precluding a rise in I/Y. But these are short-run phenomena.[55]

In the absence of monopoly or frictional disturbances, the long-run tendency is for Say's Law to prevail. But, whereas in Neoclassical theory the rate of interest determined the allocation of income between consumption and investment, in Kaldor's model a change in the real wage rate is the equilibrating mechanism.

The policy implications of Kaldor's long-run model are Keynesian:

> Unemployment, fluctuations and growing concentration in the ownership of property are not, however, in my opinion inevitable features of capitalist development. . . . Western Socialists like myself . . . believe that with suitable controls we can secure continuing full employment, a steady development of productive forces and the gradual reduction in economic inequality at the same time—without any sudden or revolutionary change in social and political institutions which could be viewed as a liquidation of capitalism.[56]

A rise in government expenditures counteracts the depression, and the system is put back on the path of balanced growth, which is defined in Kaldor's most recent work as one where 'the percentage rate of growth of capital and the percentage rate of growth of output are equal'.[57] For, Kaldor

[55] 'Alternative Theories of Distribution', *op. cit.*, p. 232.
[56] 'Capitalist Evolution and Keynesian Economics', *op. cit.*, p. 246.
[57] A Model of Economic Growth', *op. cit.*, p. 266.

argues, if output increases more rapidly than capital, the rise in the rate of profit induces additional investment. On the other hand, if capital increases more rapidly than output, the fall in the profit rate chokes off investment. From which Kaldor concludes that the economic system

> . . . tends towards an equilibrium rate of growth at which the natural and the warranted rates are equal, since any divergence between the two will set up forces tending to eliminate the difference; and these forces act partly through an adjustment of the 'natural' rate, and partly through an adjustment of the 'warranted' rate.[58]

Depression is no longer caused by a growth rate in excess of a natural rate (as in Harrod's model and in Kaldor's earlier model); rather

> . . . when rising capital-output ratios and falling profit rates cause the rate of investment to shrink at some critical speed (or below some critical level) the fall in income generated in the investment-goods industries will react unfavourably on the level of demand in the consumption-goods industries, causing a cumulative process of contraction in incomes and employment.[59]

Kaldor is correct in rejecting the thesis that depressions are caused by the actual growth rate exceeding the natural or maximum feasible rate, since the available evidence is to the contrary. In the United States, for example, employment in manufacturing rose during the prosperous 1920s by less than one-half of one per cent. Nor is there any evidence of specific bottlenecks. But Kaldor's thesis that depressions are caused by a sharp rise in the capital-output ratio also lacks confirmation. True, the immediate effect of a depression, i.e. prior to a write-down of capital values and during the period in which investment goods are still in the pipe-line, is to raise the capital-output ratio. But this rise in the capital-output ratio is a temporary effect not a cause of the depression. Data on the ratio of total capital to output for mining and manufacturing in the United States, based on volumes in 1929 prices, show a secular rise in capital-output ratios from 1870 to 1919, followed by a

[58] *Ibid.*, p. 285.
[59] *Ibid.*, p. 300.

secular decline. For manufacturing, the capital-output ratios since 1919 are as follows: 1·02 in 1919; ·88 in 1929; ·74 in 1937; and ·61 in 1948. In mining, the ratios of capital, excluding land, to output, were as follows: 2·27 in 1919; 2·14 in 1929; 1·59 in 1940, and 1·34 in 1948. Data on the ratio of fixed capital to output and to value added in manufacturing, as well as data on the ratio of plant and equipment to output in mining, exhibit the same trend.[60]

Kaldor's long-run Keynesian theory of distribution rests on two crucial and I believe unrealistic assumptions, viz. (1) the secular constancy of I/Y, since, as we saw in Chapter III, the morphology of growth of an industrial market economy requires a secular rise in the overall I/Y ratio, $dI \equiv dP_1 + dW_1 > dC \equiv dP_2 + dW_2$; and (2) the thesis that the market price of labour-power has risen and remained above its supply price since sometime in the latter half of the nineteenth century in Western industrialized countries. Further, Kaldor's explanation of cyclical phenomena is inconsistent with the data.[61] In what follows, I shall attempt (1) to apply the disaggregated Keynesian model to the Great Depression of 1929; and (2) to relate this cyclical phenomenon to the morphology of growth of capitalism, as developed in the preceding chapter.

The Great Depression:
Writing twenty-five years after the event, Galbraith points out:

> The causes of the Great Depression are still far from certain.
> . . . The twenties by being comparatively prosperous established no imperative that the thirties be depressed. . . . Nor was the economy of the United States in 1929 subject to such physical pressure or strain as the result of its past level of performance that a depression was bound to come. . . . In 1929 the labour force was not tired; it could have continued to produce indefinitely at the best 1929 rate. The capital plant of the country was not depleted. In the preceding years of prosperity, plant had been renewed and improved. . . . Raw materials were ample

[60] Simon Kuznets, *Capital in the American Economy*, National Bureau of Economic Research, Princeton, 1961, p. 209. Unfortunately, there is no sectoral disaggregation of capital-output ratios. Incidentally, the capital-labour ratio more than tripled during the period 1869–1955, *Ibid.*, p. 64.

[61] Kaldor, himself, has pointed out that '. . . meaningful generalizations about the real world can only be reached as a result of empirical hypotheses, and not by *a priori* reasoning'. *Essays on Value and Distribution*, p. 2.

for the current rate of production. Entrepreneurs were never more eupeptic. . . . Finally, the high production of the twenties did not, as some have suggested, outrun the wants of the people. During these years people were indeed being supplied with an increasing volume of goods. But there is no evidence that their desire for automobiles, clothing, travel, recreation, or even food was sated. On the contrary, all subsequent evidence showed (given the income to spend) a capacity for a large further increase in consumption. A depression was not needed so that people's wants could catch up with their capacity to produce. . . . What, then, are the plausible causes of the depression? . . . The most likely reason is that business concerns, in the characteristic enthusiasm of good times, misjudged the prospective increase in demand and acquired larger inventories than they later found they needed. As a result they curtailed their buying, and this led to a cutback in production. . . . The proof is not conclusive from the (by present standards) limited figures available. Department store inventories, for which figures are available, seem not to have been out of line early in the year. But a mild slump in department store sales in April could have been a signal for a curtailment.[62]

During the prosperous twenties, costs were falling while wages, salaries and prices remained comparatively stable. Galbraith suggests that the shift to profits may have been a basic factor leading to the Great Depression:

A large and increasing investment in capital goods was . . . a principal device by which the profits were being spent. It follows that anything that interrupted the investment of outlays—anything, indeed, which kept them from showing the necessary rate of increase—could cause trouble. When this occurred, compensation through an increase in consumer spending could not automatically be expected. The effect, therefore, of insufficient investment—investment that failed to keep pace with the steady increase in profits—could be falling total demand reflected in turn in falling orders and output. Again there is no final proof of this point. . . . However, the explanation is broadly consistent with the facts.[63]

On the other hand, Terborgh, who rejects the Keynes-Hansen

[62] John Kenneth Galbraith, *The Great Crash*, 1929, Cambridge, Mass., 1955, pp. 176–80.

[63] *Ibid.*, pp. 180–1.

stagnation thesis of a chronic tendency towards oversaving in a mature capitalist economy, makes the following points:

> . . . let us turn to the question of oversaving in 1929. In the first place, since oversaving is simply underspending, as manifested in a falling national income, *there was none before the downturn began.* The appearance of oversaving was synchronous with the reduction of spending. Secondly, oversaving did not *cause* the decline in spending; it *was* the decline. As such it explains nothing, but is instead the very thing to be explained. The real question is why spending fell off, a question we certainly cannot answer by invoking a synonym for the movement itself.[64]

However, Terborgh is unable to explain the Great Depression. In fact, Terborgh commits the same error for which he indicted the stagnationist school. According to Terborgh, a monistic explanation of the Great Depression is impossible. But Terborgh's pluralistic explanation includes such synonyms as 'the ups and downs of business confidence', 'swings in speculative sentiment', 'fluctuations of inventories', and 'other "maladjustments" too numerous to mention'.[65]

Terborgh, however, did make a prophetic remark, buried, it is true, in a footnote, viz.

> We may add, incidentally, that if World War I suspended the sword of Damocles for a full decade, the present war, with its vastly greater accumulation of deferred investment, should suspend it for an even longer period. An obvious inference this, but of course too cheerful for a stagnationist.[66]

What, then, caused the Great Depression? According to Keynes, a crisis arises because of a 'sudden collapse in the marginal efficiency of capital'.[67] Here, again, it would appear that a synonym has been substituted for an explanation. Keynes attempted to be more specific in the following:

> . . . it is an essential characteristic of the boom that investments which will in fact yield, say, 2 per cent in conditions of full employment are made in the expectations of a yield of, say, 6 per cent, and are valued accordingly. When the disillusion comes, this expectation is replaced by a contrary 'error of pes-

[64] George Terborgh, *The Bogey of Economic Maturity*, Chicago, Illinois, 1945, p. 183.
[65] *Ibid.*, pp. 186–7.　　　　[66] *Ibid.*, p. 189, n. 3.
[67] *The General Theory of Employment Interest and Money*, New York, 1936, p. 315.

simism' with the result that investments, which would in fact yield 2 per cent in conditions of full employment, are expected to yield less than nothing; and the resulting collapse of new investment then leads to a state of unemployment in which the investments, which would have yielded 2 per cent in conditions of full employment, in fact yield less than nothing.[68]

Keynes assumed that as the economy approached full employment, the marginal efficiency of capital fell. But for the period from 1923 to 1929, the evidence does not support a downward trend in the rate of profit.[69]

A 'sudden collapse in the marginal efficiency of capital' explains nothing. Rather, the problem is to explain the 'sudden collapse'.[70] Eschewing monetary explanations, i.e. relegating such phenomena to a secondary degree of importance, are we forced then to conclude *à la* Galbraith that a shift to profits necessarily implies that *ex ante* saving must be greater than *ex ante* investment? Apart from the difficulty of empirically substantiating the thesis, theoretical objections can be adduced. A shift to profits does not *per se* mean that *ex ante* saving will exceed *ex ante* investment. If the economy is experiencing a secular boom in the producer goods sector—mills to make more mills—then investment and growth will be facilitated. Conversely, if the bulk of the producer good sector's output is destined for the consumer sector, a shift to profits will result, in a comparatively short period, in a crisis of over-production originating in the consumer goods sector.

What was the pattern of investment during the prosperous twenties? United States' statistics do not provide a breakdown along the lines demanded by our disaggregation of the Keynesian system. (Indeed, although capitalism is a system of production for profit, United States national income statistics

[68] *Ibid.*, pp. 321–2.
[69] Joseph A. Schumpeter, *Business Cycles*, Vol. II, pp. 830 ff. cf. also Joseph M. Gillman, *op. cit.*, p. 100.
[70] 'The opinion is widespread that Keynes has explained what determines the volume of employment at any given time, and that our knowledge of the causes of variations in employment is now sufficient to enable government to maintain a stable and high level of national income and employment within the framework of our traditional economic organization. . . . Unhappily, this opinion reflects a pleasant but dangerous illusion.' Arthur F. Burns, 'Economic Research and the Keynesian Thinking of Our Times', *Twenty-sixth Annual Report of the National Bureau of Economic Research* (June 1946), reprinted in Arthur F. Burns, *The Frontiers of Economic Knowledge*, Princeton, 1954, pp. 4–5.

subsume residential housing under investment! Even worse, some theorists on the consumption function speak of consumer investment in consumer durables!) Nevertheless, the data available do suggest that a crisis of over-production originated in the consumer sector. However, prior to a consideration of these data, it is important to emphasize (1) that our equilibrium condition for balanced growth requires that wage payments and entrepreneurial consumption expenditures of sector I must grow *pari passu* with investment expenditures in sector II; and (2) using a different notation, Marx emphasized:

> The fact of capitalist production therefore excludes the possibility of IIc being equal to I ($v + s$). Nevertheless it might occur even under capitalist production that in consequence of the process of accumulation during a preceding number of periods of production IIc might not only be equal, but even greater than I ($v + s$). [In our disaggregated model, investment in sector II would exceed worker and entrepreneurial income of sector I.] *This would mean an overproduction in II and could not be compensated in any other way than by a great crash, in consequence of which some capital of II would be transferred to I.*[71]

I know of no available data with which to test the hypothesis that investment in sector II exceeded the sum of entrepreneurial and worker income in sector I by the end of the prosperous twenties. However, I believe the available data establish a strong case for the thesis that investment in sector II greatly exceeded wage payments and entrepreneurial consumption expenditures of sector I.

Lacking the statistical breakdown required for our model, our task would be formidable if it were necessary to obtain and compare growth data for the two sectors. However, if it can be demonstrated that sector II was experiencing a rapid growth in investment and output while simultaneously wage payments fell or remained almost constant in sector I, we would have the strongest possible case.

Statistics on total capital in the major branches of manufacturing show that from 1919 to 1929 total capital (in 1929 dollars) increased from 46,094 millions to 63,292 millions, or by about 37 per cent. Capital in the manufacture of consumer

[71] *Capital*, Vol. II, p. 608, my emphasis.

goods followed the same trend. True, the increase of capital in food and textiles was somewhat below the average, being 26 and 21 per cent respectively. On the other hand, capital in motor vehicles; printing, publishing and allied industries; and tyres and tubes increased 40, 75 and 60 per cent respectively.[72] In lieu of a detailed attempt to allocate production, employment, and investment to the consumer and producer sectors, we can gain some idea of the pattern of investment in manufacturing from the table on page 147.

The output of capital goods increased more than consumption goods; however, durable and non-durable consumption goods increased more than capital goods. This suggests that investment in consumer durable and non-durable goods was rising sharply. The impact of the automobile not only contributed to the increase in durable goods but largely sustained the growth of consumer non-durables (gasoline and lubricating oil). The growth of the automobile industry also led to increased investment in service industries:

> The automobile, the growth of recreation, and the wider distribution of purchasing power led to an expansion of the occupations that rendered services rather than produced goods. The net income originating in these occupations grew from 6·1 billion in 1919 to 11·3 billion in 1929. The number of persons engaged in them (employees being included on a full-time basis) increased from 12·2 per cent of the total in the country in 1919 to 15•6 per cent in 1929. This category excludes transportation, trade, finance, and government employment, but includes such things as garages and service stations, professional employments, barber shops and hairdressers, and domestic servants.[74]

The following chart on sales and capitalization in the consumer and producer goods sectors indicates a boom in the consumer sector.[75]

In the consumer goods industries, capital increased from about 4,300 millions in 1922 to about 6,200 millions in 1928, or by about 44 per cent; whereas, sales increased from about

[72] United States Bureau of Census, *Historical Statistics of the United States*, Washington, D.C., 1960, p. 412.

[74] George Soule, *Prosperity Decade*, New York, 1947, p. 151.

[75] Ralph C. Epstein, *Industrial Profits in the United States*, National Bureau of Economic Research, New York, 1934, p. 182. Data on the consumer sector cover 26 industries. Data for the producer sector cover 18 industries.

Index Numbers of Physical Volume of Production of Consumer and Producer Goods[73]

Year	Foods*	Other Non-durable Consumption Goods†	Durable Consumption Goods‡	Consumption Goods, Total Including Residential Construction	Capital Equipment Including Non-residential Construction and Public Works
1922	100	100	100	100	100
1923	106	121	127	111	125
1924	107	129	120	110	112
1925	106	132	140	120	132
1926	110	149	151	125	147
1927	110	159	136	124	143
1928	113	171	154	130	145
1929	113	185	172	131	170

* Foods include 'Flour, meat products, poultry products, fruits and vegetables, truck crops, milk, butter, ice cream, beverages (value series), sugar, tobacco, cottonseed oil, fresh fish'.

† 'Six series make up "other non-durable consumption goods". These relate to the production of gasoline, manufactured gas, anthracite coal, druggists preparations (a value series), kerosene, and to the consumption of newsprint.'

‡ Durable consumption goods include automobiles, furniture, electrical equipment (vacuum cleaners, washing machines, and electric refrigerators), carpets, phonographs and radios, and pianos.

[73] Frederick C. Mills, *Economic Tendencies in the United States*, National Bureau of Economic Research, New York, 1932, pp. 270, 274, and 280.

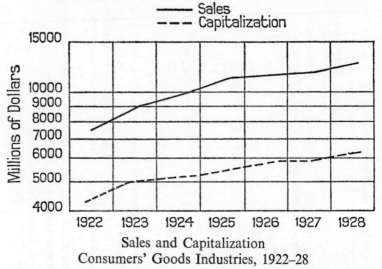

Sales and Capitalization
Consumers' Goods Industries, 1922–28

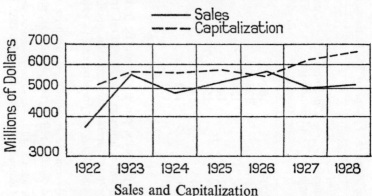

Sales and Capitalization
Producers' Goods Industries, 1922–28

7,500 millions in 1922 to about 13,000 millions in 1928. In the producer goods sector, capital increased from 5,000 millions in 1922 to about 6,600 millions in 1928, or by 32 per cent. It is not without interest that from 1923 until almost the middle of 1926, capital in the producer sector remained constant.

Data on the percentage of net income to capitalization for selected consumer and producer goods sectors also indicate a boom in the consumer sector:[76]

[76] *Ibid.*, p. 181.

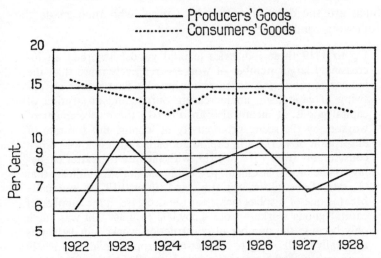

Percentage of Net Income to Capitalization
Producers' Goods and Consumers' Goods Industries, 1922–28

Such data as are available for investment, physical volume of output, sales, capitalization and net income all support the thesis that the prosperous 1920s was primarily a boom in the consumer goods sector. Let us now consider the employment data for the capital goods sector:[77]

Displacement of Labour in Capital Goods Industries, 1914–29

	Number of Workers Employed			
	1914	1919	1923	1929
Machinery	575,000	960,000	850,000	975,000
Iron and Steel	435,000	600,000	625,000	615,000
Other Metal	170,000	215,000	210,000	220,000
Transport Equipment	395,000	840,000	545,000	435,000
Stone, Clay, Glass	185,000	155,000	195,000	220,000
Lumber Products	215,000	215,000	235,000	220,000
Totals	1,975,000	2,985,000	2,660,000	2,685,000
Construction	1,492,000	1,078,000	1,162,000	1,400,000
Mines and Quarries	310,000	296,000	*	263,000

* Not available.

[77] Lewis Corey, *The Decline of American Capitalism*, New York, 1934, p. 291.

149

Such are the data presented by Corey, who then made the following comments:

> Up to 1919 these industries [capital goods] absorbed an increasingly larger number of workers, relatively more than the industries producing consumption goods. That meant an upswing of capitalism, an increasing output and absorption of capital goods. It meant also an offset to the displacement of workers by the rising productivity of labour. But the rate of absorption of workers in capital goods industries slowed down considerably from 1914 to 1919, with the rate thereafter changing to one of displacement. . . . While the statistics indicate that the rate of absorption was at a standstill in 1919–29, it actually became one of displacement; for the decrease in the number of capital goods workers from 4,359,000 to 4,348,000 was small only because the number of construction workers in 1919 was unusually small owing to the war-time drop in building. In 1929 the number of construction workers was *below* the 1914 level. . . . If construction is omitted, the number of capital goods workers fell from 3,281,000 in 1919 to 2,948,000 in 1929. The loss was wholly in transport equipment and mining, but with employment stationary, although labour was relatively displaced, in other industries. These other industries in the past absorbed increasingly more workers and the production of transport equipment was for a time the most important element in the accumulation of capital. . . . In the epoch of the upswing of capitalism the number of industrial workers grew constantly. In particular, the capital goods industries *absorbed* more workers than the industries producing consumption goods; but now they *displace* more workers. In manufactures, in 1919–29, the decrease in capital goods workers was 300,000 or 10 per cent, in consumption goods workers 138,000 or 2 per cent. This complete reversal of previous trends took place when the American economy was still on the upswing, although the rate of expansion was downward; it now becomes the creator of an increasing surplus population of unemployed and unemployable workers. *For it not only means that the productivity of labour is rising more than production, but that technological displacement of workers is aggravated by the downward movement of production, particularly in capital goods.*[78]

[78] *Ibid.*, pp. 291–3. In a footnote, Corey adds that 'In all industrial countries . . . the number of workers in capital goods industries tended to decrease from 1920 to 1929'. p. 292, n.

It was stated that if it could be shown that employment in the capital goods sector fell while investment continued to rise in the consumer sector, we would have a strong case for the Marxian explanation of the 1929 crash. Recognizing the limitations of the data, the evidence indicates that between 1919 and 1929 investment in the consumer goods sector rose sharply while employment was declining in the capital sector. Data for the period 1923–29 are not so conclusive. Nevertheless, a comparison of employment data in the capital sector with physical output of consumer durables and non-durables for the period indicates that employment only increased by about 7 per cent; whereas, the output of consumer durables and non-durables rose more than 35 per cent.

Further, investment data for the producer and consumer sectors indicate that investment in the consumer sector grew more than in the producer sector. Such being the case, wage payments and entrepreneurial consumption in sector I would have to increase more than in sector II.[79] Now we have no data on entrepreneurs' consumption; however, employment data indicate that the equilibrium condition was not fulfilled.

Ad hoc comments on the genesis of the Great Depression stress the depressed state of agriculture during the prosperous twenties. The decline of employment and income in the agricultural sector is consistent with our model since a large amount of agricultural output is constant capital. Hence, part of the labour displacement in agriculture should be added to the unemployment data in the capital goods industries. Another *ad hoc* comment stresses the great increase in consumer credit during the prosperous twenties. Although our analysis was a non-monetary one, nevertheless, the growth of consumer credit can be recognized as aggravating the tendency towards over-production of consumer goods. Again, writers on the Great Depression emphasize the shift to profits during the prosperous twenties. This also is consistent with our model in that rising unemployment in the capital goods sector coupled with a shift to property income, where the propensity to con-

[79] 1. $dP_1 + dW_1 > dP_2 + dW_2$ Since sector I must grow more rapidly than II.
2. $daP_1 + dbP_1 + dW_1 > daP_2 + d\beta P_2 + dW_2$ since $a + b = 1$; and $a + \beta = 1$
3. If $daP_2 > daP_1$
4. Then $dbP_1 + dW_1 > d\beta P_2 + dW_2$.

sume is lower, further reduces the demand for consumer goods. Data allocating production and employment between the producer and consumer sectors are not impossible to obtain.[80] Nevertheless, in general, United States statistics do not provide the requisite breakdown. One might explain the failure of statisticians to attempt to test the Marxian hypothesis *as an indication of an anti-Marxian bias*. On the other hand, the problem of ignorance also looms large inasmuch as volume II of *Capital* receives but scant attention from professional economists. Further, writers of business cycles textbooks, in their discussion of Marx, generally confine themselves to noting that Marx suggested (in volume I) that the ten-year business cycle could be related to the life of durable capital goods. In short, the contribution of Marx in volume II is generally ignored.

Marx, of course, did not accept Say's Law of Markets:

> Nothing can be more childish than the dogma, that because every sale is a purchase, and every purchase a sale, therefore the circulation of commodities necessarily implies an equilibrium of sales and purchases. If this means that the number of actual sales is equal to the number of purchases, it is mere tautology. But its real purport is to prove that every seller brings his buyer to market with him. . . . No one can sell unless some one else purchases. But no one is forthwith bound to purchase, because he has just sold.[81]

Nevertheless, Marx was prepared to utilize provisionally Say's Law in order to elucidate the additional constraints for balanced growth. It is this additional constraint (along with others previously mentioned, e.g. that in general labour still receives a cost of production wage and hence all taxes cannot be shifted to labour) that is overlooked when it is argued that 'capitalists earn what they spend; whereas, workers spend what they earn'. For example, Domar has suggested, half facetiously but half seriously, that if entrepreneurs can only be induced to invest all would be well:

---

[80] Charles A. Bliss (*The Structure of Manufacturing*, National Bureau of Economic Research, New York, 1939, p. 19) presents data for 1929 only on the producer and consumer sectors.

[81] *Capital*, Vol. I, p. 127.

Theoretically speaking, the issue is this: we have found that if firms were 'somehow' induced to invest a sufficient amount, so that national income rose at the required rate, *no disappointments would follow*. Suppose now that it were possible for the government to guarantee that income would actually grow at this rate for some time to come. Would not this guarantee, if taken seriously by the business public, call forth sufficient investment and thus *make* income grow at the required rate? This is full employment by magic. . . . On a more serious and practical level, this much can be said for the argument. Past depressions do exert a profound influence on business thinking, and an assurance that they will not recur would undoubtedly brighten the future and make many marginal projects worth undertaking.[82]

But investors were optimistic just prior to the Great Depression. *En passant*, the preceding line of reasoning suggests that the thermometer governs the weather.

Neither the Marxian theory of a tendential fall in the rate of profit nor the Keynesian explanation of a 'sudden collapse in the marginal efficiency of capital' specifically explain the Great Depression. The shift to profits during the prosperous twenties, which is stressed by students of the period, is evident from the following equation and data: $P/O = 1 - (C/O + L/O)$, where P/O is the share of profits in output (income), and C/O and L/O are the *capital-output* and *labour-output* ratios, respectively. Now Kuznets' data show a *fall* in the capital-output ratio and a *rise* in the *capital-labour* ratio for the 1919–29 period.[83] Thus, $dO/O > dC/C > dL/L$ therefore both the capital-output and labour-output ratios fell, hence the rise in P/O.

Concerning the Marxian theory of a tendential fall in the rate of profit, it is important to emphasize two points: (1) Marx constantly referred to the theory of the falling rate of profit as a secular not a cyclical tendency; (2) By the early 1860s Marx had worked out provisionally the conditions for reproduction; however, it was not until the 'seventies that the argument was further developed. Hence, Marx's equilibrium growth model was not given that strategic importance in the exposition that it warranted.

[82] Evesy D. Domar, *Essays in the Theory of Economic Growth*, p. 119. The first emphasis was added.
[83] Kuznets, *op. cit.*, pp. 64 and 209.

Formally considered, crises can 'originate' in either sector 1, producer goods, or sector 2, consumer goods. That is, we cannot conclude from the absence of the equilibrium condition, $aP_2 = bP_1 + W_1$, the line of causality. However, if entrepreneurial and worker consumption expenditures in sector 1 exceed investment expenditures in sector 2, a price rise and/or increased output of consumer goods occurs. Conversely, if entrepreneurial and worker consumption expenditures in 1 are less than investment expenditures in 2, deflation and/or decreased output occurs in sector 2. The latter, it has been argued, was the cause of the Great Depression. Further, it would be incorrect to attribute the origin of depressions to a profit squeeze in sector 1 resulting from a labour shortage. The thesis is not a legitimate interpretation of Marx's position which stresses the importance of the industrial reserve army. Further, such an interpretation would be inconsistent with the available data.

The prosperous twenties can be related to the morphology of growth of an industrial capitalist economy, which culminates in capital saturation. The period from 1896 to 1918, as Schumpeter emphasized, was one in which all government budgets were increasingly war budgets. Government expenditures not only substitute for investment but 'induce' (i.e. subsidize) additional investment. Instead of the old $C_1 - C_2$ ratio, our formula should be $C_1 + G/C_2$. The subsequent post-World War I retreat from militarism reduced this ratio. Excess capacity in the capital goods sector, an outgrowth of militarism, is characteristic of the prosperous twenties.[84] A war-generated backlog of consumer demand coupled with large investments in the production of consumer durable goods were the sustaining forces. But stagnation in the capital goods industry, the displacement of labour in this sector, meant that worker and entrepreneurial consumption expenditures failed to rise *pari passu* with investment in the consumer sector. It was this disproportionality that generated the Great Depression.

Subsequently, the rise in unproductive government expenditures brought us out of the Great Depression. But the limited welfare expenditures of the New Deal did not suffice.

---

[84] For data on excess capacity see J. Steindl, *Maturity and Stagnation in American Capitalism*, Oxford, 1952.

Further, it was not until the remilitarization of the economy that Roosevelt became acceptable to the capital goods industry. Some three or four months after Pearl Harbour full employment was achieved.

Similarly, the prolonged post-World War II period of relative prosperity in the United States can be attributed to (1) a war engendered backlog in the demand for capital goods, both at home and abroad; (2) large military expenditures by the Federal government; and (3) a vast increase in unproductive expenditures at the state and local level. The employment data are tabulated overleaf.

Thus, in the period from 1950 to 1960, total non-agricultural employment increased by 9,125,000. (Employment in agriculture declined from 7,497,000 in 1950 to 5,723,000 in 1960). *On a most conservative basis*, i.e. considering only employees in government, finance, insurance and real estate, over one-third of the increase (3,259,000) was in unproductive labour.

Our post-World War II prosperity has fostered the belief, also current in the 1920s, that great depressions (not recessions) are a thing of the past. Further, the Malthus-Keynes emphasis on effective demand provides the rationale for a point of view which, as we have seen, minimizes or ignores the cost side of the equation. In short, modern economists either ignore the distinction between productive and unproductive labour, or assume that the costs of unproductive labour (the tax burden and expenses of circulation) can be shifted to the working class, thus eliminating any threat to profits.

Now it is undoubtedly true that in the short-run, real wages can be reduced. But this does not eliminate the dilemma of capitalist accumulation. On the contrary, as we saw in Chapter III, the fall in real wages may aggravate the dilemma. It all depends on the pattern of investment. Thus, if the boom is due to heavy investment in the consumer sector, a fall in real wages leads to inadequate demand for the output of the consumer sector.

On the other hand, if prosperity is the result of heavy investment in mills to make more mills, the fall in labour's share in national income is beneficial to accumulation. During the period in which investment achieves temporary independence from consumption, a fall in labour's share provides greater

L* 155

156

Annual Average of Employees in Non-Agricultural Establishments
(in Thousands)

Year	Total	Mining	Contract Construction	Manufacturing	Transport & Public Utilities	Wholesale & Retail Trade	Finance Insurance & Real Estate	Service & Miscellaneous	Government
1950	45,222	901	2,333	15,241	4,034	9,386	1,919	5,382	6,026
1960	54,347	709	2,882	16,762	4,017	11,412	2,684	7,361	8,520

(Source: United States Department of Commerce, Statistical Abstract of the U.S., 1962, p. 219.)

profits for further accumulation. But we have seen that investment can achieve only temporary independence from consumption: First, because the specificity of capital equipment
means that investment is directed to a particular type of output
and not, as Dobb pointed out, to 'a stream of demand stretching to an infinite future'. Secondly, even if we ignore the
specificity-of-capital-equipment constraint, there is a ceiling
on the ratio of producer to consumer goods. Ultimately, a
point would be reached where profits would be insufficient to
purchase the output of the producer goods sector. And this
could happen, as Grossman pointed out, even if the rate of
profit were high. Thus, given a boom in the producer sector,
the fall in labour's share in national income would be an insufficient offset to the shortage of profits. Further, if part of the
burden of increased unproductive expenditures falls on the
profit-takers, the dilemma is aggravated.

In other words, the Keynesian-Kaldor model contains two
incompatible assumptions, viz. (1) a secular fall in real wages
or at least a decline in labour's share in national income and
(2) secular full employment, given Keynesian fiscal and monetary policies.[85] We are now in the world of Say's Law of
Markets; only government is the *deus ex machina* that insures
effective demand. Productive workers subsidize unproductive
workers. This, of course, will not raise labour's propensity to
consume; rather it would be a case of robbing Peter to pay Paul,
given the assumption that workers' propensity to consume is
unity. Nevertheless, since labour's share is falling, consumption
expenditures will decline relatively. Now given the fact that
sector 1 must grow more rapidly than sector 2 and that
investment can only achieve temporary independence from
consumption, what guarantee is there that a crisis of over
production originating in sectors 1 or 2 will not recur? That is to
say, *even with full employment*, there still remains a basic
problem, the Marxian condition for balanced growth or sectoral equilibrium. The absence of overall planning characteristic of a market economy or the so-called mixed economy,
so popular with modern economists, contains no mechanism

---

[85] In the unlikely case of secular full employment coupled with a secular fall
in real wages, I would conclude that this would lead to a labour shortage!

for the correct allocation of capitalists' expenditures that will insure balanced growth.

The preceding analysis raises an interesting problem concerning the future of capitalism. Will the demise of capitalism be 'not with a bang but a whimper'? Are catastrophic events foreshadowed? Or will we grind imperceptibly towards that stationary state envisioned by Ricardo? One cannot answer the question dogmatically. It might be possible to increase government expenditures, even at some expense to the capitalist class, and thus maintain sufficient employment to avoid another Great Depression. Abstractly considered, the Malthusian panacea of sacrificing accumulation (growth) to employment appears possible. But this, I believe, is only an abstract possibility which ignores the specifics of capitalist accumulation, viz. automation, capital-saturation, and the impossibility of reconciling planned growth with a market economy.[86]

The past seventeen years of relatively full employment are but a short slice of time in the history of capitalism. True, the greatest depression and the most destructive war in history have been followed by a prolonged period of world capitalist prosperity. But time is running out. The inevitable tendency towards excess capacity is again apparent. The industrial reserve army rises secularly. Capital export continues. The competitive struggle for foreign markets has been intensified. Because the ratio of investment to consumer goods must rise, the dilemma remains—either insufficient profits to continue the process of investment; or, given a boom in the consumer sector, the fall in labour's share in national income during prosperity precipitates a crisis of over-production in the consumer sector. Further, because of the long-run tendency to continually substitute capital for labour, each boom leads to a higher ratio of investment to consumer goods. And this requires a greater depression to correct the imbalance.

[86] cf. *Has Capitalism Changed*: An International Symposium on the Nature of Contemporary Capitalism (edited by Shigeto Tsuru), Tokyo, 1961.

APPENDIX*
CLASSICAL ECONOMICS AND THE
DUESENBERRY HYPOTHESIS

It remains true that, taking man as he is, and has been hitherto, in the western world the earnings that are got by efficient labour are not much above the lowest that are needed to cover the expenses of rearing and training efficient workers, and of sustaining and bringing into activity their full energies. Alfred Marshall, *Principles of Economics.*

INTRODUCTION

Divergent assumptions about the degree of human rationality differentiate theories of consumer demand and saving. On the one hand, we have theorists who postulate rational consumers capable of long-run planning to maximize consumption utility throughout a lifespan.[1] On the other hand, we have the Duesenberry thesis which, like Veblen's, stresses cultural conditioning and non-rational psychic states as determinants of consumer behaviour.[2]

Superficially it might appear that one must choose between the above alternative theories, viz. either we accept a theory of human behaviour that postulates a fine degree of human rationality and prevision; or we are forced to embrace a theory

---

* Reprinted by permission of the Western Economic Association, Proceedings of the Thirty-Fifth Annual Conference, 1960.

[1] e.g. Franco Modigliani and Richard Brumberg, 'Utility Analysis and the Consumption Function: An Interpretation of Cross-Section Data', *Post-Keynesian Economics*, ed. Kenneth Kurihara (New Brunswick, N. J., 1954). Similarly, in the 'permanent income hypothesis' consumption utility is maximized over a longer than normal time-span. Milton S. Friedman, *A Theory of the Consumption Function* (Princeton, 1957).

[2] James S. Duesenberry, *Income, Saving and the Theory of Consumer Behavior* (Cambridge, 1952).

159

heavily burdened with psycho-cultural postulates for the economic explication of consumer behaviour.

But the necessity of accepting either alternative constitutes a false dilemma. One can agree with Veblen's strictures on the limitations of marginal utility analysis while simultaneously refusing to accept as adequate the Veblen-Duesenberry theory of consumer behaviour.[3]

In the following discussion, I assume the validity of Veblen's critique of marginal utility analysis; and, also, recognize its applicability to such theories of consumer demand as have been articulated recently by Friedman, Modigliani and Brumberg.[4] However, the Veblen-Duesenberry positive theory of consumer behaviour with its emphasis on invidious comparisons is rejected on methodological grounds as discussed below.

THE DUESENBERRY HYPOTHESIS

Duesenberry's theory of consumer demand rests on the following psychological and cultural propositions:[5]

(1) Everyone wants to improve the quality of the goods he uses for any purpose (p. 25).

(2) The fundamental psychological postulate underlying our argument is that it is harder for a family to reduce its expenditures from a high level than for a family to refrain from making high expenditures in the first place (pp. 84–5).

(3) . . . the basic source of the drive toward higher consumption is to be found in the character of our culture. A rising standard of living is one of the major goals of our society (p. 25).

(4) Duesenberry further concludes that past consumption habits exert an inertia effect on buying patterns. However,

---

[3] Thorstein Veblen, 'The Limitations of Marginal Utility', reprinted in *What Veblen Taught*, ed. Wesley C. Mitchell (New York, 1945).

[4] They attempt to build up a simple model of rational consumption or saving behaviour by assuming that a basic reason for saving in any period is to smooth out (though not necessarily equalize) consumption over a planning period which is longer than the conventional annual accounting period. Both formulations, it should be noted, treat net investment in consumers' durables as saving rather than consumption.' Irwin Friend and Irving B. Kravis, 'Consumption Patterns and Permanent Income', *Papers and Proceedings of the American Economic Association*, May 1957, p. 537.

[5] Duesenberry, *op. cit.* Subsequent references in parentheses are to this work.

Appendix

inertia is overcome by the 'Demonstration Effect' which in turn is implemented by invidious comparisons sustained by inferiority feelings (pp. 26–8).

(5) In general, an individual's utility index is a function of the ratio of his expenditures 'to those with whom he associates' (pp. 32 ff.).

From the above postulates, Duesenberry derives the following conclusions:

(1) the aggregate savings ratio is independent of the absolute level of aggregate income.

(2) the aggregate savings ratio is dependent on (a) interest rates, (b) the relation between current and expected future incomes, (c) the distribution of income, (d) the age distribution of the population, (e) the rate of growth of income.

(3) Because of the discontinuity in preference functions the aggregate savings ratio will be rather insensitive to changes in interest rates, expectations, and preference parameters. Large changes in these factors will be required to produce substantial changes in the savings ratio.

(4) *Cet. par.* the propensity to save of an individual can be regarded as a rising function of his percentile position in the income distribution. The parameters of that function will change with changes in the shape of the income distribution (p. 45).

Next, Duesenberry considers the empirical findings on consumption and savings that, he believes, are consistent with the preceding deductions; viz. data on income aspirations and satisfactions, a comparison of Negro and white savings, comparisons between savings in different cities and income groups, and long-run changes in savings.

The cross-section attitudinal data on 'Income Satisfaction and Income Aspiration' are consistent with the Duesenberry hypothesis. The data indicated that as income rose there was a percentage increase in the number of satisfied individuals and also that the percentage increase in income required by dissatisfied individuals to achieve satisfaction tended to fall.[6] However, an exception occurred among those receiving the

---

[6] R. Centers and B. Cantril, 'Income Satisfaction and Income Aspiration', *Journal of Abnormal and Social Psychology*, January, 1946. Cited by Duesenberry.

highest weekly income (over $100 weekly). Here, although the numbers expressing dissatisfaction continued to fall, those individuals who remained dissatisfied indicated a desire for a much greater percentage increase in income: 'This phenomenon is explained by the authors of the study by the fact that the dissatisfied members of the over $100 group have a higher social status than is indicated by their income' (pp. 48–9). The reason advanced by Centers and Cantril and accepted by Duesenberry is that among the higher income group are many professional people whose social status exceeds their income: i.e. professional people identify socially with the upper group but recognize that economically they are outside this group. Further,we are informed that inferiority feelings are more prevalent among the children of the professional group, and from this it is boldly inferred that the same holds true for the parents of these children. For the present we shall note only that Duesenberry says nothing about the ratio of income of professional people to their cost of living (including, of course, the cost of reproducing a similar grade of labour-power).[7]

Duesenberry finds that empirical data on Negro and white savings also indicate that the absolute level of income is not a determinant of consumer behaviour. Rather, the data show that consumption and saving are a function of the individual's relative position in his particular community (pp. 50–2). Further, although data on savings and incomes for individual cities do not prove the hypothesis, 'our hypothesis is not inconsistent with the observations' (p. 54). Similarly, the long-run stability of the consumption function indicates that 'the savings ratio is independent of the absolute level of income' (p. 57). Again, savings cannot be dependent on the real income level since the break even point (in 1941 prices) rose from $800 in 1917 to $1500 in 1935–6 (p. 78).

Duesenberry finds that for 10 per cent of the population 'consumption is dependent on current income relative to past income as well as on the absolute level of current income' (p. 86). For the other 90 per cent of the population the absolute

---

[7] Of course, it is possible that an unfavourable ratio of income to costs for a particular group might engender not only dissatisfaction but also 'inferiority feelings'. However, the difficulty inherent in an appeal to psychological states for an explanation of economic phenomena is that of an *embarras de richesses*.

level of income is not a determinant of consumption expenditures. This leads Duesenberry to conclude that a rise in income will not in itself raise the aggregate savings ratio; however, 'the savings ratio *may* be increased by equalization measures' (p. 45).

Although the data adduced by Duesenberry are consistent with his intragroup emulation hypothesis, the theory is based upon certain cultural and psychological postulates concerning the nature of modern man in an industrialized society. But there is no economic explanation of 'culture'. Rather, in philosophical terms, culture is a primitive concept not susceptible to further analysis. Thus culture is a *deus ex machina* requiring no economic explanation. Further, the analysis leans heavily on psychology. 'Emulation', 'invidious comparisons' coupled with 'inferiority feelings' are strategic factors in the Duesenberry theory of consumer behaviour. In turn, these psychological states are either sustained or nurtured by the cultural mileu.

Now there is no harm in recognizing that economic phenomena have their epiphenomenal correlates; however there is a danger in substituting these epiphenomenal correlates for economic data in an economic analysis. After all, there is no guarantee that *different economic phenomena may not have almost identical epiphenomenal products.*

In effect, Duesenberry's theory *eschews an economic explanation of economic phenomena.* Nothing is said regarding demand for labour; nor of the long-run supply-price of labour-power; nor of the ratio of income to cost of the commodity labour-power. Instead recourse is had to putative psychological states of inferiority feelings that determine not only the behaviour of professional people but also partly explain the consumption patterns of 90 per cent of the population. It is in this sense that Duesenberry's theory of consumer demand constitutes a sharp break with classical economic analysis.

AN ALTERNATIVE HYPOTHESIS

It is true that classical political economy was characterized by implicit psychologizing. Individualism, psychological hedonism, utilitarianism and some degree of rationality were the implicit and sometimes even the explicit postulates of the classical school.[8] Further, such assumptions about the nature of man dictated a categorical imperative, viz. the establishment and preservation of a society consonant with man's nature.[9]

But given these psychological assumptions, classical political economy operated on the objective level of the market. By way of analogy, psychological assumptions were relegated to the wings; whereas, the market was the stage wherein the plot unfolded. Pursuing the analogy, the protagonists were capital accumulation, diminishing returns in agriculture, and demand and supply balanced at a point where cost of production equalled market price. Thus an increased demand for any commodity, including labour-power, led at first to a rise in market price which, in turn, resulted in an increased supply that tended to restore market price to cost-of-production price. Land, not being a commodity, was the notable exception. That is to say, having made its bow to psychology, classical political economy proceeded in its analysis of economic phenomena without further recourse to psychological states.

As I see it, although economics may take cognizance of man's psychological predispositions, human nature is largely a product of the social order.[10] Thus, the economic analysis must proceed to a consideration of those economic developments that not only necessitate a specific pattern of social behaviour but ineluctably determine its continued existence, e.g. the long-run stability of the consumption function.[11] In this writer's opinion, the realm of economic necessity has its own special competence. This suggests that by minimizing psychological interpretations of the data, economists will be

---

[8] Veblen's insistence on the importance of the hedonic calculus in both classical and marginal utility analysis fostered in him 'the preconception (which was a misconception) that marginalism and classical political economy were essentially identical'. Eric Roll, *A History of Economic Thought* (3rd ed.; Englewood Cliffs, N. J., 1956), p. 443.

[9] cf. W. Stark, *The Ideal Foundations of Economic Thought* (London, 1948), pp. 48–50.

[10] cf. Erich Fromm, *Man for Himself* (New York, 1947), esp. pp. 67 ff.

[11] *'When, then, the explanation is undertaken, we must seek separately the efficient cause which produces it and the function it fulfills.'* Emil Durkheim, *The Rules of Sociological Method* (Glencoe, Ill., 1950), p. 95.

Appendix

in a better position to appreciate the advantages inherent in their own discipline.[12]

Our alternative hypothesis accepts the dictum of the classical school that demand for labour governs supply and, as a corollary, that labour-power is paid a 'subsistence' wage.[13] However, as I have argued elsewhere, subsistence must not be interpreted as a bare physical minimum of food and shelter; but rather subsistence must mean the cost of producing a more highly skilled, educated and more intensively utilized labour force.[14] *The strategic variable for consumer behaviour is the ratio of income to cost of labour-power.*

Consider first the data on the long-run stability of the consumption function. Obviously Duesenberry is correct when he states that consumption is not determined by the absolute level of real income. But it does not follow from the data that we must accept Duesenberry's hypothesis that an individual's consumption pattern is determined by his relative position in the income distribution. Rather the data on the long-run stability of the consumption function are consistent with the thesis that in general, even in contemporary society, labour receives a cost-of-production wage.

Similarly, short-run changes in the propensity to consume are a function of the ratio of income to cost of labour-power. *Cet. par.*, in periods of prosperity (depression), the propensity to consume falls (rises). But this is a case in which the ratio of income to cost of labour is favourable (unfavourable) because changes in the average cost of labour power are secular rather than cyclical.

[12] '*The determining cause of social fact should be sought among the social facts preceding it and not among the states of individual consciousness.*' *Ibid.*, p. 110. *En passant*, it may be remarked that although it is still too early to determine the duration of the comparatively recent 'interdisciplinary' fad, it should be obvious by now that the results of this 'co-ordinated approach' are frequently eclectic rather than synthetic.

[13] That Marshall accepted the classical view is evident from the quotation at the beginning of the paper. Whereas, in the Ricardian model the value of labour-power rises as a result of diminishing returns in agriculture; for Marshall, the increase in the long-run supply price of labour reflects the cost of rearing 'efficient' labour.

[14] See my *Population Theories and the Economic Interpretation* (London and New York, 1957), esp. Ch. VIII, 'Demand for Labour'. At the time of writing this book I was chasing a different hare and did not consider *explicitly* the implications of my theory *vis-à-vis* other theories of consumer demand.

Appendix

Our strategic variable, the ratio of income to cost of labour-power, also explains population dynamics. By means of this ratio it is possible to reconcile apparently contradictory demographic findings: viz. in the short-run (cyclically speaking) fertility varies directly with income; however, in the long-run fertility varies inversely with income. The paradox of declining fertility concomitant with rising real income vanishes once it is realized that *the secular rise in real income was accompanied by a long-run rise in the supply price of labour-power.*

In the following diagram, *hypothetical secular* data are utilized to illustrate how the ratio of income to cost of labour-power determines both consumption and fertility:

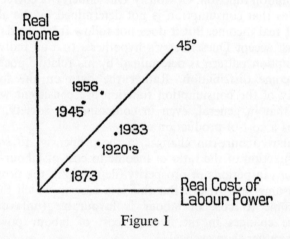

Figure I

To the left of the 45 degree helping line, the income cost of labour-power ratio is favourable to fertility and some savings. To the right the opposite is the case. At the aggregate level, a fall in the average propensity to consume results from a rise in real income unaccompanied by a rise in the average cost of production of labour-power.

The significance of the ratio of income to cost of labour-power is evident also when we consider the other data adduced by Duesenberry to confirm his hypothesis. In the following diagram we disaggregate labour-power and utilize a cross-sectional rather than an historical approach to explain inter- and intra-occupational differences in fertility and savings:

166

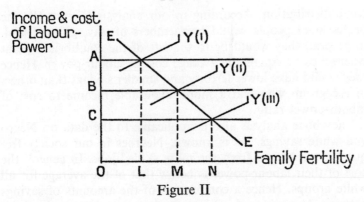

Figure II

Let OA equal the average cost of labour-power for grade I, OB for grade II and OC for grade III. Curves Y (I), Y (II) and Y (III) represent the distribution of incomes for each grade of labour-power, respectively. OL is the average number of children for group I, OM for II and ON for III. The graph is consistent with demographic findings; e.g. the EE line shows the traditional inverse relation between fertility and income.[15] The graph also indicates that when income is above or below the average cost of labour-power for a particular grade, fertility varies directly and not inversely with income. Further, it is possible that the fertility of some fortunate members of a highly skilled group (I) may exceed that of certain less fortunate members of a less highly skilled group (II). Finally, the graph suggests that beyond a certain point the supply of children becomes perfectly inelastic to income changes. *If* this point could be reached, saving would greatly increase. Prior, however, to reaching this point there would be increased saving along with increased fertility (compare Figure I).

Consider now the data on 'Income Satisfaction and Income Aspiration' that Duesenberry believes confirms his theory of the importance of an individual's relative position in the in-

---

[15] N.B. The EE line runs from northwest to southeast so that in equilibrium the average fertility of skilled labour is less than that of unskilled. One explanation of this phenomenon is differential mortality. That is to say, the required supply of labour is realized through differentials, in both mortality and fertility. *Cet. par.*, fertility varies directly with mortality. This proposition not only follows theoretically but is consistent with demographic findings on differential mortality. For a summary of these findings see *ibid.*, p. 186, n. 2.

come distribution. According to our analysis (Figure II), the professional people would be members of, say, group I and, in general, they would be to the left of the equilibrium point where income equals the average cost of labour-power. Hence they would have lower fertility and smaller savings than others in the group who had a more favourable income to cost of labour-power ratio.

The above analysis also is applicable to the data on Negro and white savings. As is known, Negroes in our society frequently are barred from the more skilled jobs. In general the cost of their labour-power is below that of the average for all white groups. Hence a comparison of the amounts of savings between Negroes and whites at the same income levels is misleading. It is necessary to standardize for occupation. A Negro with the same absolute level of income as a white 'enjoys' a more favourable ratio of income to cost of labour-power, simply because he is barred from the better jobs. In the above diagram he would appear to the right of the equilibrium point for group III.

The argument that in general labour receives a cost-of-production wage is consistent with demographic findings and the data on the long-run stability of the consumption function. The analysis also explains short-run (cyclical) phenomena. In periods of prosperity the ratio of income to cost of labour-power is favourable. But this is also a period characterized by increased fertility and increased saving (e.g. life insurance) for those whose income is derived from the sale of labour-power of one type or another. The opposite holds in periods of depression.

Regarding those individuals in society whose income is derived from ownership, the situation is materially different. Such individuals are not subject to commodity-type analysis; nevertheless, there is a role for them in classical economics, i.e. one of saving and investing.

CONCLUSION

In presenting our alternative hypothesis it has been argued that data on consumer behaviour are explicable in terms of market analysis, and that this is possible with a minimum of recourse to psychology. Further, the classical hypothesis provides not only a theory of consumer behaviour but also one of population growth. The classical hypothesis is more general in that population is not (as in the Duesenberry model) an exogenous influence, but rather a dependent variable as is, of course, the propensity to consume.

Finally, with respect to policy implications if the classical analysis is correct, then one of Duesenberry's conclusions is suspect; i.e. the proposition that income equalization measures will increase the propensity to save. Rather the analysis indicates that the effects of redistribution measures will be determined by the ratios of income to cost of labour-power for different groups.

INDEX

Index

171

Index

172

Index

173

Index